Chris,

Thank you
energy you
the commun
It has been so incredible
working with you and
inspiring our youth to use
their voices and experiences
to create change.
  I look forward to
seeing all the amazing things
you will be doing for
Grande Prairie and all
the people you will inspire
along the way.

much Love & Light
CaraJones
2018

ng

.rie.

# DEAR COLE,
# NEVER SAY NEVER

*A Spiritually Intuitive, Artistically Optimistic,
Story of Overcoming Adversity
& Living a Fulfilling Life*

# CARA JONES

**BALBOA.**
PRESS

A DIVISION OF HAY HOUSE

Balboa Press books may be ordered through booksellers or by contacting:

Balboa Press
A Division of Hay House
1663 Liberty Drive
Bloomington, IN 47403
www.balboapress.com
1-(877) 407-4847

Because of the dynamic nature of the Internet, any web addresses or links contained in this book may have changed since publication and may no longer be valid. The views expressed in this work are solely those of the author and do not necessarily reflect the views of the publisher, and the publisher hereby disclaims any responsibility for them.

The author of this book does not dispense medical advice or prescribe the use of any technique as a form of treatment for physical, emotional, or medical problems without the advice of a physician, either directly or indirectly. The intent of the author is only to offer information of a general nature to help you in your quest for emotional and spiritual well-being. In the event you use any of the information in this book for yourself, which is your constitutional right, the author and the publisher assume no responsibility for your actions.

Any people depicted in stock imagery provided by Thinkstock are models, and such images are being used for illustrative purposes only.
Certain stock imagery © Thinkstock.

ISBN: 978-1-4525-7388-5 (sc)
ISBN: 978-1-4525-7395-3 (hc)
ISBN: 978-1-4525-7389-2 (e)

Library of Congress Control Number: 2013908081

Printed in the United States of America.

Balboa Press rev. date: 05/14/2013

# DEDICATION

This book is dedicated to every woman who has ever doubted her magnificence. You are creators, innovators, leaders and earth angels. Continue to let your light shine.

To my parents: for never giving up, breathing life and potential into each obstacle and for creating an eternal optimist.

To my son, Cole: thank you for teaching me about continuous learning, in miracles and for choosing me to be your mommy. I love you.

# THANK YOU

To my editor Paula Lowe, I couldn't have done this without you.
You truly are an earth angel.

To my illustrator Rita Vantassel, I always knew that you would
be creating the image for my first book and our years together at
NSCAD University taught me so much about joy, talent
and embracing our artistic selves. Thank you.

CO-PUBLISHED BY

# THERESA MACDONALD AND LIANNE CAMPBELL

Words are not adequate to express the gratitude I feel towards my co-publishers, Theresa MacDonald and Lianne Campbell, two realtors with Remax Realty in Antigonish, Nova Scotia. This mother-daughter team has continually supported me on my journey, whether through giving me my first job, cheering me on from the sidelines or making an extremely generous donation to see my book published. These women are amazing.

When working with young women, I often reflect on the strength and leadership I see demonstrated in leaders and entrepreneurs like Theresa and Lianne, and I strive to inspire those young women like they have inspired me.

Thank you again, Theresa and Lianne, for your ongoing support and for always believing in me and my vision.

# ACKNOWLEDGEMENTS

Supporters

I want to thank two very special supporters of my book by telling you something special about each one of them.

Allen MacHattie was a high school classmate of mine and, in the intensity of my experience living life with epilepsy and never truly feeling beautiful, Allen always broke through that insecurity by reminding me how truly beautiful I am. This was not an easy task and, as the years flew by, Allen always showed his support for me with his genuine personality and continual encouragement. Thank you, Alan, for believing in my vision and for always being a great friend.

Dennis Fagundo and I met in my first year of art school. He was one of the engineering students living in the dorm. Combining art students and engineers in a living environment was never boring. Dennis, my fun-spirited friend from Bermuda, who liked to call me "kid," always stood out in my life. He encouraged me to work and live inspired and to be unafraid of motorcycles (thanks for all the tours around Halifax). All these years, later he continues to help me in any way possible, including helping me publish this book. Thank you for being a great friend and always cheering me on; your generosity will never be forgotten.

# A Special Thank-You

My editor Paula Lowe is an amazing talent. Not only has she taught me so much throughout this process but her endless support and life altering conversations I will cherish. I could not have done this without you.

Rita Van Tassel, my illustrator, has been one of my best friends since our second year in university. Never have I ever laughed so hard than in the presence of this woman and her fun-loving personality.

Rita and I lived together in my final year of art school and after deciding to have a party, Rita, ambitiously hand drew and coloured our party invitations. The illustrations of us were so amazing that I kept the invitation all these years with the intent that if I ever wrote a book, Rita would illustrate the cover.

Thank you Rita, for your support and your amazing illustration. It means the world to me.

# CONTRIBUTORS

Thank you to all the amazing contributors who supported my book and made donations to see it in print. Your support is invaluable.

Caren Anderson
Lisa Burns
Terry Cameron
Vivian Hanifen
The Sisters of Saint Martha
Liz Millet
David King
Stephen King

# INTRODUCTION

After my near-death experience at the age of six, life was never the same. Often times I felt a sense of loneliness and frustration being back in this body and taking on whatever purpose I was meant to fulfill. At the same time, I felt blessed to be given the gifts of empathy, intuition and the unwavering determination to live life with meaning.

When I arrived home from Australia in 2004, pregnant, single, and my future unknown, I realized I had to let go of all preconceived notions from the past. Everything that I had been told I would never achieve I had successfully accomplished.

Growing up with a severe epileptic condition, my quality of life was often compromised. I was told I would never graduate high school, never attend university and possibly never live past my early twenties. Yet there I was, twenty-six years old, a high school graduate, a university graduate and world traveler about to become a mother.

From the outside, I could see why my situation appeared less than ideal and maybe a little scary. A single mother, in debt, with no support from the father, living in a small economically challenged community—not exactly a winning combination.

Although normal doubts and fears of becoming a mother took over, the calming sense of destiny overshadowed these emotions. I had done everything I set out to do in life against all odds. How was becoming a mother any different?

We all have adversity in our lives. Some people endure hardship which seems unfathomable to others, yet they survive. They not only survive, but often thrive and succeed in ways that seem miraculous.

I don't pretend to understand why we struggle, but I do know, without a doubt, that even in the most challenging circumstances the four principles that continue to shine through each individual's experience are faith, hope, perseverance and resilience.

These themes consistently ripple throughout this story that I have written to my unborn child. I hope that one day, when he is a man, he will not only learn from my experiences he will grow to understand that there is more to life than our physical eyes will ever see. We create our joy and, no matter what obstacles we face in life, nobody can control our joy. I hope that he will learn that anything is possible, that people make mistakes and that forgiving yourself is the most challenging, but rewarding, obstacle of all. I pray that he will always have faith in himself and will, "never say never."

**February 13, 2004**

**Dear Cara,**

    **You are one girl I know who will put this to good use. Write your little heart out. I hope you have a wonderful trip, learn lots, meet great people and have a blast.**

    **I'll miss you, but know we'll be in touch, and you'll be back before we know it. Remember, the most important thing is to have fun . . . while being careful.**

**Love, a friend always**
**Karen**

# CHAPTER ONE

# MY LITTLE KANGAROO

June 12, 2004

Dear Cole,

Well, I did have a good trip and I ended up bringing home the biggest gift to remember Australia by. I brought home you. I am going to keep this journal for you so that one day you will get a glimpse of what your mother was like at 26. I'm sure when you're older, and you read this, it might be hard to imagine me as young, but I am and I look forward to all the lessons you will teach me over the years. Most of all, I look forward to meeting you.

Right now, I am a month-and-a-half along and you are only the size of a penny, but I talk to you every night, vowing to take care of you and hoping you will choose to stay in my body. I've only been back in Canada for a day and, for the first time in years, I truly mean it when I say, "It feels good to be home."

I guess I will fill you in on how you came to be.

I went to Australia in February of 2004 to do my first apprenticeship in wood sculpture with artist John Beasley. I had the idea that if I went somewhere exotic and international people would open the door for me. Little did I know how much I would learn in the rain forest and how only about ten percent of it would be related to art.

During my time there, I was forced to let go of many of the burdens I carried around and fear I had lurking in the corners of my heart. One of those fears was being alone with my thoughts.

The very first night I arrived in Australia, John and his wife, Ruth, invited me into their dining room for supper. As I sat at the table, enjoying the hot

1

soup they had prepared, my eyes wandered the room and stopped dead at a site that made me question if I had made the right decision in choosing Australia. There on the wall was a fairly large gecko and right beside it was a spider the size of a small dinner plate. I could see its hairy legs from where I sat and, in that moment, I felt I might have made a huge mistake.

John looked over to where I was staring and smirked.

"Oh, don't worry," he expressed in his thick Aussie accent. "He's only a baby."

"A baby," I thought. "Dear Lord, I really don't want to meet its mother!"

My cabin was nestled in the rain forest behind John's house. I was alone with snakes, rats, lizards and spiders. I felt very proud of myself by the second week as I actually started getting used to it all. This was huge considering the last thing John said to me on the night of my arrival was to make sure I wore thongs to the washroom because in the night baby scorpions could get in under the door.

Well, I wasn't quite sure what he meant. Was I supposed to wear skimpy underwear to the washroom to protect myself from scorpions? Then my Canadian brain kicked in and I realized that is what he called flip-flops. Duh!

I began learning very quickly and John really kicked my ass when it came to my idea of art. The first few days he made it very clear that he was going to have to undo everything art school had taught to me. "You all come here the same," he said, "thinking the idea comes first and the technique, second. Well, I do things the old way, so from now on you will have to relearn everything."

In my naive, fresh-out-of-art-school mind I resented that comment, but I came to understand quickly what he meant. You see, in art school I had many ideas—really great ones. My professor, Lorianne, got a glimpse of my idea book and told me that I had to make sure I protected it. She explained that there were many artists who could not come up with half the original concepts I did and would be happy to steal from me. That professor was right and just before I left school I experienced this firsthand when I went into a gallery. One of the girls I had spoken to about my great idea went ahead, took the idea, and presented it in a solo show. I remember how devastated I was, but there was a huge difference between her and me that I didn't realize at the time. Yes, she was a thief, but she knew how to implement the ideas.

In my last semester of art school, I got the best critique on a piece of work I had ever received. I had created a performance piece called "A day in the life of my two breasts." I walked around the city with cameras on my breasts and took photos randomly while someone filmed me. I was pointing out to the world that my gender was only a fraction of my experience as an artist and person and, if I were to hand my gender a camera, the pictures would come out distorted and fuzzy.

She told me my work showed genius, but I could not survive on genius alone, as my work had a rushed, last-minute feel about it. She was so right. My work did have a rushed feeling about it and I never finished what I started. John was determined to fix that, but he had a tough job ahead of him. He constantly called me a "seven," and I got so fed up with it that one day I finally asked him what the hell he was talking about. John had studied art therapy and one of the things they learned was the Enneagram which categorizes people's personalities. He had me nailed as a seven and shook his head one day at how he always got sent the same personality type for these apprenticeships. I asked him for one of these books on the Enneagram so I could see what he was talking about and that night became engrossed in what I learned.

# Seven
## THE ENTHUSIAST
## Enneagram Type Seven

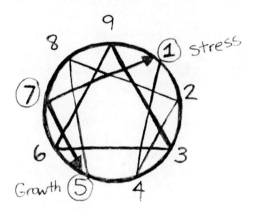

### The Busy, Variety-Seeking type:
### Spontaneous, Versatile, Acquisitive, and Scattered

### Type Seven in Brief

Sevens are extroverted, optimistic, versatile, and spontaneous, often playful, high-spirited, and practical, they can also misapply their many talents, becoming overextended, scattered, and undisciplined. Sevens constantly seek new and exciting experiences, but can become distracted and exhausted by staying on the go. They typically have problems with

3

impatience and impulsiveness. *At their Best*: they focus their talents on worthwhile goals, becoming appreciative, joyous, and satisfied.

**Basic Fear:** Of being deprived and in pain
**Basic Desire:** To be satisfied and content—to have their needs fulfilled
**Enneagram Seven with a Six-Wing:** "The Entertainer"
**Enneagram Seven with an Eight-Wing:** "The Realist"
**Key Motivations:** Want to maintain their freedom and happiness, to avoid missing out on worthwhile experiences, to keep themselves excited and occupied, to avoid and discharge pain.

Oh, my God, he was right! As a spiritual person, this was the first time I had read anything so accurately detailing my personality that it shook my belief system for about a week. Truthfully, I was devastated! How the hell did this book and this system know me so well; wasn't my soul my soul? Wasn't I unique? The Enneagram book even stated that I had three books on the go and was accurate about what subject matter I was reading. How was that possible?

I marched into the wood shop the next day and expressed my frustration to John about not wanting to be a seven! John, with that sly grin, kept sanding his sculpture and, under his breath, said, "Typical seven-thing to say!"

The biggest statement that really rang true for me was that it called me an experience junky, always seeking the next high. This rung true in my heart and I hated it. Lorriane's critique popped into my head and her worry for me that I never completely finished anything. Was it my destiny to continue to live this way? God, I prayed that this was not the case. It was the beginning of my unravelling and, Cole, without that unravelling, I might not be able to have the small amount of confidence I do now to proceed with this job of creating life and following through.

# CHAPTER TWO

# ALONE WITH MY THOUGHTS

June 13, 2004

Dear Cole,

Things were going well in Australia for me. I spent my days sanding all of John's sculptures by hand as he introduced me to the different tools for carving. He helped me get over my fear of the chainsaw, somewhat, but I knew it was something I was going to have to face if I wanted to actually create a sculpture. I sat there sanding for hours, my headphones blasting out tunes that kept me in rhythm. It was the perfect way for me to learn to be with myself.

After work, I would retreat to the cabin for a night of reading and reflection. This is where the spiritual side of me became stronger than I had ever experienced.

I was doing Reiki almost every day and my pain and heartache bubbled to the surface. Your mother does not have a good track record with men and had allowed them to burden her heart with their irresponsible actions. I realized that, for the past two years, I had been walking around the world with a void in my heart. I felt I had so much love to give, but didn't have anywhere to fully direct it.

I believe it all began as a child for me, but the trait grew worse and my teenage years approached. You must understand, my Sweet Child, that your mother has had an interesting experience, thus far, in the lessons of life.

We all have our adversities, and I am always reminded that so many other people are worse off. My adversity had caused a deep-rooted insecurity in me on many levels. Although I am extremely optimistic and believe in love, I often failed to believe in love when it came to loving me. I spent the majority of my pre-teen and teenage years wearing a mask to cover my fear—my fear of dying, not experiencing, not learning and never being . . . in love.

I guess the path to all of this began when I was five years old and I introduced my brother and my mother to my imaginary friend, Dini. I remember it as if it were yesterday.

## **<u>My Imaginary Friend</u>**

"He's standing right there," I announced with great conviction. "Can't you see him?" My brother, Chris, and my mother, Coleen, just stood there and tried not to smirk too much as I so seriously introduced them to a being made of thin air. "Cara, sweetheart, there's nobody there," my mother soothingly confirmed. I couldn't understand it. How could they not see him; he stood so tall and beautiful.

I had been seeing Dini for months. The meaning of his presence was unclear to me, but I loved having him around. Our conversation was limited, as if we didn't have to use words to know what each other were thinking. I suspect now, looking back, that Dini was a visitor preparing me for what was yet to come.

I was only five years old when he first showed himself to me. Shortly after, I remember strange things started happening to my body. The first time it happened, I was lying in bed, staring at my floral-print wallpaper, when the room suddenly started to feel (what I described at the time) as "fat." Each time it happened, fear crept up onto my skin and buried itself in my soft flesh. I remember Dini always being there with a smile in his eyes which made me feel such ease afterwards, but soon the episodes grew worse.

One day, while acting out Snow White in my best friend, Laura's, basement she watched me fall to the floor, thrashing and gasping for breath. Laura, thinking I was playing, giggled as she observed my silly additions to the story. These episodes had become such a common occurrence that they never fazed Laura nor me, too young to understand the depth of what was happening. My parents started to notice my strange behaviour as well. One time, in particular, walking into the mall, I felt the sensation creep up on me. I tried to control it, but it was no use, my legs lost all control. I watched the walls of the department store grow lucid and alive, my tongue, thick and heavy, stood between me and my ability to communicate. My mother tried to hold me up; she used everything in her power to support me, but her daughter was falling away from her in more ways than one.

Dini remained with me this whole time. He would observe from the corner with his gentle and loving presence. I knew that no one could see him, but I was so relieved that he made himself visible to me, especially during school. I began to find that keeping up the charade of everything being adequate in my world was a bit exhausting. Dini was the one thing that gave me strength when the abuse started to happen.

Mrs. Talbot, my grade-one teacher, didn't understand. To her, I was just a spoiled child seeking attention. Falling to the floor, staring into air when she asked me a question, were all signs of a brat trying to be one above the rest. The only way she knew how to deal with me was to punish me. Soon my lunch was taken away. I stood in the corner more than I sat at my desk. Her eyes became so cold and her voice became coated with resentment towards me.

So shy and introverted, I couldn't understand why a grown-up hated me so much. All I wanted to do was make her happy so I never told my parents about any of the things she did to me; I wanted to protect her. Dini explained to me in his own way that she needed love, most times, I found loving her an unbearable challenge.

It was a cold December day and all the students had just returned from playing outside, each face showing the rosy complexion of a Nova Scotian winter. You could hear the hustle and bustle of each classroom preparing for the big Christmas concert for our parents. Mrs. Talbot suggested that we practice our song in front of the grade-two classes before our big debut the following week. I was so excited and so extremely nervous. We all considered the grade-two class the big kids and I had a huge crush on a boy named Jason who would be sitting right there with his eyes on me. As we lined up, I stood tall, ready to give a perfect performance. When I looked up and spotted Jason in the second row, I blushed at the very sight of him. The music started and we all began belting out our heartfelt Christmas carol when I felt that familiar feeling starting to possess my body. My body started sinking to the floor, my eyes stayed focused on Jason, and I tried fighting my legs, with all my might, but it was no use; the feeling was stronger than my five-year-old will. I lay completely flat on the ground, looking up at Mrs. Talbot, who was now leaning over me with a stern look of disapproval painted across her middle-aged face. She grabbed my arm and tried yanking me up to my feet, to no avail. "Get up, Cara," she demanded, trying to keep her temper to a dull roar in front of the other teachers. All the children were giggling and I prayed to God to make me vanish, but God didn't answer. Mrs. Talbot decided to teach me a lesson for my disobedience and, when I finally gained control and was able to stand, she slapped my butt three times in front of the whole class as a warning to them not to cross her.

Dragging me to our classroom across the hall, she continued to torment and accuse me of maliciously making a fool of her and the rest of the class. Tears streamed down my delicate cheeks as I stood in the corner the remainder of the day, praying to God to make it stop and for Mrs. Talbot to like me again. In the unconventional way that God likes to work, he answered my prayers.

It was three days after the incident at school and I had caught the flu so I stayed home to recuperate. The day after my experience with Mrs. Talbot, my mother and father sat me down to ask me all kinds of questions, desperate to find answers. What was happening to their little girl? I tossed and turned, playing and trying everything to get them to talk about something else. I had no idea what was happening to me and I sure didn't want Mom and Dad to worry about me so I just decided not talking about it was the best answer.

After spending the day comforting me from the effects of the stomach virus, Mom finally got me settled into a good night's sleep. Quietly, she crept out of the room, gently closing the door behind her. Mom went into the living room where my dad was on the sofa. As they sat intertwined, the light from the television flickered, revealing the tired expressions on their faces. A loss for words left the couple quiet and hypnotized by the imagery flashing before them. They relaxed in the calm and in an instant the storm arrived with a bang.

"What was that?" Mom bolted up at the sound of a thud against the wall. Feet not touching the ground, she threw open my door to find me in a catatonic state, my face turning various shades of blue, gasping for air. "Dear God, Fran, quick." Dad, already behind her, ran to the phone and called our neighbour, a registered nurse who happened to be off duty.

"Cara, sweetheart! Mommy's here. Wake up, baby," my mother repeated as tears gathered in the corners of her eyes. "Mom, what's wrong with Cara?" my brother, Chris, inquired as he peered into the room in shock at the sight of me. "Honey, go back into your room. Your sister's going to be okay. We just need to take her to the hospital so she will feel better." The terrified look on Chris' face was enough to put my mother over the edge.

As soon as the neighbour arrived, she ordered my father and mother to help her get me into the car, fearing I would not survive waiting for an ambulance. Dad, with super strength and unwavering determination to save his little girl, lifted my stiff body as if it were stuffed with feathers. Securing me in the car, mom continued to call out my name while Dad ran every red light all the way to the hospital. Upon arrival, I was whisked away to emergency where nurses and doctors attempted to suction me and bring me back from the flat-line state I had slipped into after drowning in the fluid that so quickly filled my lungs. For a few minutes, I was dead.

# CHAPTER THREE

# My View from the Ceiling

I heard the door close as Mom left my room and, for a moment, sleep felt close by. Soon that feeling was replaced with a rapid wave of terror. When my eyes adjusted to the darkness in the room, I saw Dini standing in the corner. He told me not to be afraid and that soon I would return. With the end of that message I found myself rising and watched the situation unfold from the ceiling of my room. I felt no pain, no fear, only lightness as I observed my parents trying to bring me out of my catatonic condition.

Dini remained close; I could feel others with him and had an understanding of all that was occurring. I watched the doctors work tirelessly on me, determined to revive the limp, precious six year old who lay before them. Soon, as quickly as I had floated away from that shell, I was slammed back into it, all lightness exchanged with heavy pain. My head throbbed, fear was back and confusion overcame me as I tried to figure out who I was, who they were, where I was and what had just happened to me.

Sleep overcame my body like a wave for the next two days as I drifted in and out of seizures. They rushed me to Halifax for treatment. Dini was gone and I never saw him again. As if he prepared me for the dramatic climax of the story, he exited stage right, instilling knowledge in me to survive and overcome all that lay before me. My six-year-old mind couldn't comprehend the miracle I had been given, but upon reflection, I was never the same again.

This was the beginning of my spiritual journey here on earth, Cole, something that has remained with me and my sense of purpose to this day. I have always felt a sense of empathy for everyone even when they wronged me like Mrs. Talbot. As I continue to share my story with you, I want you to know that people make mistakes and in those mistakes obstacles are created but it's often those obstacles and how you overcome them that become the biggest, most profound teachers in life. I hope someday you will understand what I mean, but I pray that you will understand through an experience less freckled with pain.

## CHAPTER FOUR

# THE PSYCHIC PREDICTION

July 14, 2004

Dear Cole,

Sitting here writing this journal to you, holding my belly, trying to grasp the reality that you exist, remembering those nights in Australia where I sat in deep mediation, feels like light years away from this moment. How strange that it was in those moments when I was given my first glimpse of you.

I'll never forget it. One day I went into a deep meditation after getting on my hands and knees crying to God to give me a sign. Where was my life headed? I fell asleep and had the most vivid vision. I was sitting on a table giving birth. My best friend, Karen, and my Mother were there and, every time I had a contraction, Karen would start rubbing these tattoos of flags on my leg, making me laugh. I asked her what she was doing and she said, "Well, this baby has got to know where you've been." I immediately woke up!

The feeling that embraced my body was a bliss I had never felt before. I didn't feel alone in that room. I felt love radiating off everything and the only thing I could think to do was get on my bike and drive to the store at the end of the road and devour a Mars bar. Chocolate always makes me feel fantastic!

I didn't understand the vision; it wasn't as if I wanted to get pregnant and I took it as a glimpse into my distant future. I never clued in that the vision didn't include a man in the picture. I didn't question why it was Karen and Mom. I just thought it was a reassuring sign that one day I would be lucky enough to experience the gift of life. I called Karen in Canada right away to tell her about the experience. She was one of the best friends I had and always wanted to hear about my spiritual experiences since she had witnessed them firsthand many times. It was one of those things I didn't even really know I did, but, I guess, I would get a faraway look in my eyes, blurt out something random that was going to happen and, sure enough, days later, the episode I predicted unfolded. Karen knew I had this gift even if I didn't understand it, and it was nice to be able to share with someone without her questioning my sanity.

About a week after this vision, I went into the city of Cairns with John. We had a couple of free hours so he dropped me off at the mall. I walked around, checking out all the stores and sales, when I noticed a man set up inside a smaller room and saw he was giving tarot card readings. Someone was sitting with him and I watched as he intensely spoke to this person while pointing at each card. In front of his window, he had a table with a scrapbook of all the police cases he had helped solve. I had my cards read before while living in Halifax, but I had never seen anyone with a record of using his psychic ability to help solve missing–person cases. I was completely intrigued and decided to give it a go.

I sat down in front of him and shuffled the cards. He briefly looked at them and then looked into my eyes for what seemed like an eternity. It made me uncomfortable so I let out a giggle to ease the tension. Then he asked me a question that floored me. "Cara, why aren't you doing this?"

"Doing what?" I asked, playing dumb. He looked me in the eyes again and responded, "Honey, you have the ability to do what I do. You have the sight. Why do you not use it?"

I had never had anyone ask me that before, let alone know that I experienced the things that I did, so I just told him the truth. "It scares me."

"You don't have to be scared; you could really help people with your gift. Why don't you try?" he insisted, ever so gently.

"I don't want to know," I told him. "Some of the things I see I don't understand and I'm not sure I want to."

He looked back at the cards and then at me. "Well, Cara, you can run from your gift, but you can't hide and by the time you are in your early thirties it will find you, whether you like it or not, but it won't be as scary as you think."

I was fine with that; my thirties felt like eons away and I would just deal with it when the time came. The next thing he said to me almost made me fall out of my chair.

"Are you trying to get pregnant?" he asked in a serious tone that made me feel like I was being talked to by a parent.

Cara Jones

"No," I replied quickly but I was shocked he asked me this considering I had just had one of the most profound spiritual visions a couple of days before.

"Are you sure?" he persisted.

"Umm, yeah," I responded sarcastically. "Pretty sure that's not on the top of my list, I gotta say."

He was quiet for a minute and then took my hand.

"Well, I have to warn you that, if this is something you don't want, you must be careful because in exactly four months you *will* be pregnant."

I left his little table dumbfounded. PREGNANT! Wasn't that a vision about my distant future? I couldn't even picture it and when I got in the car I joked around with John and told him what the so-called "psychic" said. The last thing I remember about that day was saying to John, "Could you imagine if that happened? How totally different my life would be?" Then I put it out of my head.

A few weeks later, I met your father and the prophecy, which I had already forgotten about, began to unfold.

# CHAPTER FIVE

# INN THE CITY

July 15, 2004

Dear Cole,

Sometimes I think about John and the Enneagram and I laugh. I was really restless and staying in the rainforest, sanding, reading and meditating, became pretty darn boring. I wanted to experience some of the fun backpacking culture that was happening down in Cairns.

The night before I left for Australia, I talked to my new best friend, Kathy, for the first time. I was sitting in my kitchen with my mother and our neighbour, Anne Marie, and she went on to tell me her niece was also going to Australia the next day. At first I didn't really care and just said, "Oh, yeah," but, when she asked me if I knew Karen Gillis, my ears perked up.

"Yes," I told her. "I went to high school with her; she was a couple of years younger." Well, Karen was also in Australia and Kathy was on her way to meet up with her. I immediately went to the phone and called Kathy to introduce myself. When she answered the phone, I remember being a little nervous and just started rambling on about how we were both on the same flight and I hoped I would meet up with her at the airport. I hung up the phone and realized I didn't even tell her my name so I dialled back and said, "Oh, yeah, by the way, my name is Cara Jones," and we both laughed.

Life has a tendency, Cole, of providing extreme cases of synchronicity. That is how I feel about my relationship with Kathy and how we met. It was destiny.

I had a brief description of what she looked like but, when I got to the airport and saw all the people, I thought that finding her was going to be like finding a needle in a haystack. I stood in one of the two lines to get my ticket and, as I walked to the ticket agent, I noticed a beautiful blond girl walking up to the booth right beside me at the exact same time. I wondered if it was her and then I noticed a girl I knew behind her, Jennifer MacDonald. I realized that it was Kathy and Jenn was her sister. Right away I went up and gave Jenn a hug and introduced myself to Kathy. The ticket agent asked if we would like to sit together and, of course, we agreed. As the two of us set off on an adventure together to Hong Kong and then to Australia, I knew in my heart this young, shy girl was part of my future.

I hadn't seen her since we got off the plane and I only knew the name of one hostel she had given me so that weekend I went to Cairns in search of Kathy.

It didn't take long to find her; she was staying in a hostel called "Inn the City." I reunited with her as well as my friend, Karen Gillis, whom I hadn't seen since high school. The two of them took me around the city. We danced at all the hot-spots and I quickly adjusted to the life of a backpacker. I gotta say, I loved it!

One night they took me to a dance bar in the rain forest where everyone bungee-jumped. This is where I met your father for the first time. His name is Jason and he was 27 at the time and worked at the hostel. We became friends and I fell for the blond hair and Aussie accent. I knew our relationship wasn't serious and I was glad for that because my heart was not ready to trust in love yet (I had been hurt so many times before). We had only been together a handful of times and I enjoyed my time with him-he knew how to make me laugh. It only takes one time when a condom breaks for your whole world to change. When it happened, I remembered lying there, knowing I had just conceived a child, but my ego dismissed it and said, "Don't be silly; you are just being paranoid."

A couple of weeks later, I grew tired of Jason's wandering eye and realized I was starting to like him way too much. When I suspected I was pregnant and couldn't get him to talk to me, I broke up with him. I knew the situation wasn't good for me. The owner of the hostel found me on a bench at 5 a.m., crying, and asked me what was wrong. When I told her what I suspected, she took me to the drugstore and purchased a pregnancy test for me. I always felt so grateful for the amazing people like Cheryl and her husband, Steve, who took me under their wings and treated me like family when I was away from my own. They are special people and I will always hold a special place in my heart for them.

The pregnancy test was negative and I let Jason know, then I caught a flight up the Gold Coast to Surfer's Paradise with the intent of experiencing more of Australia. That was too much of a close call for me and I needed to get away and clear my head.

The next few weeks I traveled and met great people and made it as far as Byron Bay. This was, by far, the coolest spot yet, with its Utopian vibe and the incredible Arts Factory hostel where I stayed. I could see why people never wanted to leave.

I learned to surf, created art, danced to drums on the shore while watching dolphins play with surfers in the waves. I should have felt the freedom there, but something felt wrong. I couldn't put my finger on it, but something was pulling me back to Cairns. I was happy to do so because, honestly, it was so darn cold in Byron Bay and I did not travel to the other side of the world to be cold. I said goodbye to my new friends and caught a flight back to Queensland.

I saw Jason the next day, nodded to him, but I avoided getting involved with his immaturity and kept my distance. That day Cheryl asked me, "Honey, did you get your period yet?"

"Nope," I replied. "It must be the weather and food making me late."

"Sweetheart, you better go get another test just to be on the safe side," she expressed with great concern.

It was super early in the morning so I had to wait for the stores to open, but I wasn't concerned. The test said negative before so I knew I wasn't pregnant. When nine o'clock rolled around, I went to the store, picked up a test and made my way to the washroom. I pulled the stick up to view the screen and, in that moment, someone as intuitive as I couldn't have predicted the shock I received when I stared at the stick and the blue plus sign appeared. What the hell! How could this happen? It said negative before. I began to panic, my heart started to race, my mind began swirling and then something happened in that stall that I will never forget.

Just as quickly as I began to panic, a feeling came over me. It felt like the air became warm and washed over my skin and melted its way to the center of my heart. I felt joy and I knew I wasn't alone in that stall. I sat in this feeling of love for what seemed like an hour and a knowing occurred: I was going to be just fine!

I opened the door and went to find Kathy.

# CHAPTER SIX

# FACING REALITY

July 16, 2004

Dear Cole,

You have to understand that your father was a very young 27 years old and was not ready to take responsibility for his actions, but I hope that by the time you meet him he will have changed. When I told Jason about you, he was sweet, and shared with me the horrific story of his last relationship. You see, you have a half brother named Jacob. The relationship that Jason was in with Jacob's mother really did a number on him. I don't think he's ever been the same.

He kissed my belly and said, "You are going to be a good mom. I know it." We didn't part on good terms. He initially reacted well but, the next night, went out and got drunk and wouldn't talk to me. I want you to know that when I told him about you he was very excited. He is a good person. Sometimes good people experience strange things and make bad choices.

When I told your grandmother, her reaction shocked me the most when she said, "I'm so happy for you." I had to make that phone call from Australia, in an Internet café and I vomited in the alleyway just before as I anticipated my parents' reactions. I never expected that reaction and, to this day, try not to question it. She told me that she believed I'd wanted to have a baby for a long time. I'm not really sure where she came up with this theory, seeing as I am a world traveler. Despite what she believes, I never planned this even though I am very happy you are here.

I would have liked you to have the "loving couple" greeting you into this world, but know that your mother will welcome you with more love than you can imagine.

My Dad was so disappointed in me, but that's a normal reaction for most fathers. It's hard enough for a dad to realize his little girl is having sex let alone the fact that she is having a baby. Plus, I know he never wanted me to have to struggle in life, but you can't protect your adult child forever.

I felt so bad for my parents when I told them the news. They had already been through so much with me growing up. They fought so hard just to keep me alive. I am so grateful for the sacrifices and love they showed me.

Remember when I wrote about my near-death experience? Well, just picture what that was like for Mom and Dad. It's something I hope, as a parent, I never have to go through with you.

# CHAPTER SEVEN

# MY MOTHERS BARGAIN WITH GOD

The week during the seizure episodes, my father stayed behind in Antigonish to take care of my brother, Chris, and Mom traveled with me to the Izaak Walton Killam Hospital for Children in Halifax. I arrived exhausted and weak, continually having seizures the whole two-hour ambulance drive to the city. As Mom sat by my side, watching me wither away, she stroked my soft forehead and swallowed her uncertainty.

Night came quickly after we arrived and the doctors informed Mom that I would be looked after in the morning and stressed the need for her to get some sleep. How could she sleep? She had just survived every parent's worst nightmare and couldn't shake the feeling that it was just the beginning of the battle. Time stood between her and sunrise. She arose and walked the halls of the paediatric ward, searching for solace. As each foot placed itself in front of the other, Mom peered into the windows of the other patients, becoming more horrified with each passing frame. Every child on the ward had a track mark through which each had been given oxygen or had been suctioned out. They were severely brain damaged, in a coma or both. As Mom made it to the end of the hallway, she found herself on her knees, weeping and talking to God. She thought of my birth mother. That woman was out there somewhere never knowing the wonderful little girl I had grown to be: the light in my eyes, my laughter and silliness, the quiet, yet empathic, nature I possessed. Right then and there my mother vowed to God that she was going to do everything in her power to keep me alive so that my birth mother would someday get to know that incredible person she had created. Wiping her tears, she returned to my room, crawled into bed with me and fell asleep, listening to the sweet sound of my breathing next to her.

# CHAPTER EIGHT

# THE BIRTH
# OF ASSERTIVENESS

July 18, 2004

Dear Cole,

My mother kept her promise to God, but the next twelve years proved to be some of the most challenging times that she and my father would face. I spent the majority of my childhood years in and out of hospitals and my parents did everything in their power to give me the best quality of life. Years later, when I talked to Mom about that time in our lives, I was in awe of the strength that both of them embodied for the love of their children.

They moved my bed into their room so they could be there if I were to have a life-threatening seizure, never knowing what each night would bring or if I would wake up in the morning.

They had an ongoing fight with the education system to give me an equal opportunity to learn, not giving up on my abilities that lived in the shadows of my condition and endless learning disabilities. They just never gave up.

There is one story, in particular, that always stands out in my mind, revealing the unflappable determination my mother displayed when it came to executing my rights.

It was shortly after my first hospitalization in Halifax that I shared with her the abuse I had suffered at the hands of my grade-one teacher. Of course, back then, I could not come close to understanding the horror my mother would have felt after receiving the information I so reluctantly shared. She only showed me her calm, collective side, but, years later, she told me what had happened and how she became transformed by the experience.

Mom came from a very strict upbringing in Guysborough, Nova Scotia. Her whole life she lived the values of a Roman Catholic and was taught that you never question authority figures. This included anyone from priests, nuns, doctors to teachers. This was an act of obedience that had been programmed into her. What would she do with the knowledge that her precious little girl had undergone such ridicule by these so-called authority figures?

Three days after returning from Halifax, my mother made her way to the elementary school. She learned that after my admittance into the hospital my teacher, Mrs. Talbot, had a nervous breakdown after learning of my near-death experience. Mom knew she had the power in that moment and all previous beliefs of authority figures flew out the window. She was going to stand up for her baby and they were going to listen.

Standing in the doorway of the principal's office, Mom's face turned various hues of red as she tried to control her anger. The sight of my mother turned the principal's complexion to ashen grey.

"I know that I have every right to sue this school and that woman for everything you've got, and it still wouldn't scrape the surface of making up for the trauma and humiliation my daughter has been through," she trailed off, her anger slowly replacing itself with compassion. "But I'm not going to do that because I know that living with that type of ignorance is punishment enough." Sitting down, her deflated inferno gave way to a calm assertiveness she had never felt in her 30 years. She basked in the high of her strength and grounded spirit. Never again would she let a projected belief come between her and the safety of her family. It was up to her and Dad now to give my brother and me the best quality of life they could provide. Her purpose became defined. She stood up and walked out of the school a completely different person.

# CHAPTER NINE

# THANK GOD FOR UNANSWERED PRAYERS

July 29, 2004

Dear Cole,

I've been home for almost three weeks now and angels continue to shine down on me, helping me every day.

It took me only a week and a half to get a job in Antigonish and the one I got was like hitting a jackpot. I'm working at the Maritime Inn as a receptionist. It ends in January, the month you are due. I receive better than minimum wage and it includes health insurance. I couldn't have asked for better luck.

I remember how hard it was for me to get a job here as a teenager. After my two brain surgeries, I went out and searched for work, eager to take on the world. I was so excited because I was seizure free for the first time in my life. I went from 100 seizures a day to none; it was a miracle. So I hit the road and handed out application after application. I had a few interviews and things were looking good, but I had done something in the meantime that hurt my chances in a town that wasn't ready to hire people with medical issues as employees. I agreed to be the lead story in the local newspaper in hopes that maybe my story would assist others going through a similar experience. The article was successful in the way I intended, but really hurt me on the job front. It seems that the only part of the story people focused on was the sentence where I said I "used to have over 100 seizures a day." Guess they sort of overlooked "used to" and only heard the 100 seizures

24

part because when I got an interview they would tell me I had the job and when to show up, then a day later I would get a call saying they couldn't hire me. I became desperate for work and even joined the odd job squad for teenagers. I finally caught a break and got a call that they needed someone for housecleaning. Another girl and I were ready to go when the head of the odd job squad called and said she needed to tell me something. I could hear the hesitation in her voice. "Cara, I am so sorry," she trailed off. "I'm not sure how to tell you this, but the people who own the house you were supposed to clean have expressed they prefer you not be in their home." I was dumbfounded. I had been discriminated against over and over and this time it really hit me in the gut. Tears streamed down my cheeks and I saved face by composing my voice in a professional manner.

"It's okay," I said to this girl, whom I knew felt terrible to have to deliver that news.

"No, Cara, it's not okay, and again I am so sorry. Please don't give up and I will do what I can for you."

"Thanks," I replied, and I never forgot her kindness. The truth was it was hopeless; I wasn't going to get a job.

As I sat on the floor, holding the phone on my lap, something occurred to me. This disappointment was a familiar feeling and there was no way I was going to let it get me down.

My teenage years were definitely full of confusion and disappointment, but I realized a couple years before that most of the disappointment was in the realization that it was other people's perceptions of what I could or could not achieve—not my own. I will never forget the moment when I realized I was going to achieve something that everyone deemed impossible.

# CHAPTER TEN

# THE BEGINNING

"Cara, wake up, honey. It's time to get ready for school," my mother's voice traveled loudly down the stairs and into my room. "I'm up! I'm up!" I responded as I crawled out of bed and made my way to the bathroom. It was a typical morning in our house; Mom and Dad hustled through the house preparing for work as my brother, Chris, and I moved in slow motion, less than eager to attend another day at school. Staring at my face in the mirror, I sighed at the perpetual appearance of pimples and wondered when I was ever going to be pretty enough for guys to notice me. Figuring it was not going to be today, I jumped into the shower and tried to change my thinking to a more optimistic approach. As I dried myself off, picked out an outfit that fit my mood best, and finished applying the last bit of makeup to cover those unsightly blemishes, I hopped up the stairs to the breakfast table and joined my family.

"Don't forget to take your pills, sweetheart," Mom chimed in as I poured myself a glass of milk. "Mom, I know. God!" I threw my morning dose of Tegretol down the hatch and inhaled a bowl of Captain Crunch. "How are you feeling this morning?" Mom asked as she moved around me to grab a cigarette from the counter. "Fine," I replied in a droning voice, hating having to answer that question what seemed like a hundred times a day. "Don't give your mother that tone, Cara. She's only looking out for you," my father interrupted sternly. I knew she was and I appreciated it, but sometimes I wondered what it would be like to go a whole day without people watching my every move to see when the ball was going to drop or if I was going to drop.

I heard the familiar sound of Mable (my best friend, Caren's, car) pull into the driveway ready to pick me up. "I'm off," I announced to my family and bolted for the door. "Have a good day, Cara, and be careful," I heard Mom calling after me in that loving, yet anxiety—driven, manner.

Sitting in the back of the car listening to my friends talk about boys and classes, I stared out the window, remembering only a year before when I couldn't go a whole car ride without the feeling of déjà vu. When déjà vu occurred, it wasn't because I was soaking in feelings of all of this happening before, it was because I was in a partial complex seizure. My body would become paralyzed, I'd feel sick and sleepy, yet, after feeling the third seizure descend, unknown to my peers, I somehow mustered the ability to contribute to the conversation. It took all the internal will I had, but, like most days, I craved normalcy and hid the severity of my condition to my friends and the world.

I had been seizure free for a year and life was great. My medications were working, my parents were less on my case and I had just written and passed my beginner driver's license. I was fitting in with my friends and feeling normal for the first time in years. I swam in the ease of it, not expressing my under-the-skin fear that it was all too good to be true.

We arrived at school just as the bell was ringing for homeroom. The hallways were alive with teenage drama: rustling paper, fast shuffling feet, the smell of boys wearing too much cologne, and rows of girls standing in front of their locker mirrors, perfecting their hair and make-up. I said goodbye to my friends and ran to my homeroom for attendance call. Reaching the doorway, I noticed Mr. Mac, my homeroom teacher, looking over some papers and my friend, Jennifer, eagerly awaiting my company in the seat next to her. As I settled into the uncomfortable plastic chair, Jennifer quickly informed me of all the news I was oblivious to after returning from a two—day hiatus due to the stomach flu.

"Did you hear?" Jennifer questioned me in her singsong voice. "Today is career day and university representatives are coming from all over to present to us. Isn't that exciting?"

I could already feel the lump in my throat forming and showed no reaction to her hyper enthusiasm.

"That's great," I replied. "Let's go down together and check it out." Jennifer agreed with a nod of her head and we were quickly dismissed by our homeroom teacher. A swarm of students spilled into the hallways eager to be at this stage in their lives, finally no longer a future goal but a distant reality.

Tables lined the hallways with three-panel presentation boards bearing the faces of smiling university students enjoying their higher education. I slowly walked by each one, stopping at St. Francis Xavier University, then Holland College and, finally, Saint Mary's, but there was a problem. Each university declared that you needed an average of 55 percent to get in and, the truth was, I was failing. I knew that the chance of me getting into any of those universities was slim to none, and I was prepared to give up on the dream of attending. What I wasn't prepared for was the feeling that accompanied these thoughts. I felt anger, resentment and jealousy towards all my friends who could easily get accepted to any of those schools. What I hated most of all was that the majority of them didn't even have to work hard for it. I felt tears beginning to well up. My friend, Jennifer, caught the distraught look on my face and checked to see if I was okay, but, before I could answer her, I saw it. It was like Moses parting the sea of scattered teenage bodies to reveal the poster that would change my life forever. It called to me and I walked towards it as if in a movie sequence where everything had been slowed down and all that stood between it and me was my limiting thoughts. It read, "The Nova Scotia College of Art and Design."

Art students freckled the poster, holding paint brushes, sculpting plaster and drawing large charcoal sketches. My insides took a leap and, for a brief moment, I felt I had pulled a Mary Poppins and jumped into the picture. In that moment I knew, like I have never known anything, that attending that school was my destiny.

## Visualizing a Dream

Upon returning home, I pulled the poster out of my schoolbag and proceeded to the junk drawer in search of tape. Placing the adhesive on each of the four corners, I scoped out the perfect spot in my room to display my new-found dream. Once it was in place, I stepped back and stared at its glowing potential, my stomach feeling alive with the idea. I couldn't wait for my mother to get home so I could share my amazing news with her. Killing time, I pulled out my sketchbook and inhaled the inspiration brought on by my future endeavour, knowing I would have to hone my skill in order to be recognized by the school's elite standards.

Before I knew it, 5 p.m. stared back at me from my clock radio and I heard my parents' car pull into the driveway. Bolting up the stairs, my feet barely touching the carpet, I lunged at my mother, pulling her towards my room.

"Come on, Mom. I have something so awesome to show you!"

As I lead her to my room, I felt butterflies in my stomach. I knew she was going to be just as excited as I was. Mom was always talking and pumping me up for the future, preaching continuously that I could do or be anything I wanted to be. What she was unaware of was her inability of hiding her fear. It was always underlined in the little things she said, such as her continuous use of the word "realistic."

I remember just one month prior, driving over the Macdonald Bridge towards Halifax, the rush of excitement as I entered the city. I stated clearly to my parents, "You know, some day I'm going to live here."

My parents glanced at each other, taken off guard by the conviction in my voice. Wanting to protect me from getting my hopes up, Mom replied, "Sweetheart, that's a nice dream, but right now it's not very realistic. Besides you probably wouldn't like living in the city; it's not all it's cracked up to be."

I knew they were wrong and I also knew what they were trying to do. A lump of disappointment formed in my throat. I shook it off and began picturing myself as one of those beautiful women walking the streets before me, free and independent. I wondered where they were walking to—maybe their cool studio apartment where they had fun city parties with their fun city friends. I knew I would live there, but I was content with only the fantasy for now.

Staring at the poster, my mother did her best at injecting enthusiasm into her voice, pulling it off as sincere. Wanting to believe her own words, she again looked me in the eye, touched my shoulders and repeated her mantra, "Sweetheart, you can do anything you set your mind to." I knew that she didn't really believe her own words, however, I chose to believe them. Her words were cultivating a "never-say-die" attitude in me that was beginning to overshadow the self-loathing inner vocabulary that whispered unheard to the outside world.

## In the Shadows

The next day, I went to school with lightness in my step. For the first time, in what seemed like forever, I could see a future for myself that extended past the age of twenty. Maybe my life had hope after all and it wouldn't all end with an obituary reading, "Woman found dead in her sleep after enduring fatal tonic clonic seizure."

I had a frequent nightmare that paralyzed me many nights. When I opened my eyes, I anticipated the interior of a coffin instead of my blue, frilly twin bed. The nightmares had become less frequent since my meds had been working and the seizures stopped. I started to dream instead of being older, having a job and maybe even a boyfriend.

A boyfriend—even the thought of it was heavenly. Someone I could truly be myself with, who would love me despite of my condition and who would, just like in the movies, sweep me off my feet, pull off my mask, toss it in the ocean and carry me off into the sunset.

My invisible mask had become a permanent part of my wardrobe. I wore it most days to cover up my persisting insecurities in a desperate attempt to appear normal among my peers. The mask had an everlasting smile; it agreed with everything and rarely revealed what lay underneath— unimaginable fear: fear of never knowing when the next earthquake would hit and how shattering it might be. Where would I wake up, who would be speaking to me, would I recognize them, would I recognize myself? I felt I did a good job maintaining these two personalities, but I was wrong and, over the years, I became ill beyond the epilepsy. The source of the illness was my own thinking. I had a deep secret. I hated myself.

My girlfriends were my shelter, but how I envied their beauty and confidence as I hid in the shadows of their outgoing natures. I was known by the male portion of my class as the tall, dark-haired girl who hung out with so-and-so. It was not an existence most people would dream of having, but it kept me safe from ridicule and misunderstanding. I would look at those insanely cute boys in my class and pray to God that one day they would look at me the way they did most of my girlfriends. They made it all seem so easy, but who was I kidding! Who would want to be with someone who looked as hideous as I did, curled on the floor in a tonic clonic seizure, drool oozing out the side of my mouth, my face purple and blue? A real catch, I'm sure.

By the end of the day my energy had shifted quite a bit and I felt like I was relapsing from the flu that I had only days prior. I was really looking forward to my second driver's education class, but cancelled when I felt my dizzy head couldn't provide the focus I needed. I couldn't believe a whole week had passed since I wrote my beginner's exam. It was such an exciting day in the Jones' household and I couldn't believe it was happening to me. I remember only two years previous celebrating this milestone in my brother's life. We pigged out on chocolate cake as Chris opened his first set of keys to my parents' car. I felt a twinge of jealousy, doubtful that I would get to experience such a milestone, yet, two years later, there I was. It was a high for me unlike any other I had experienced to that point. Getting my license was a symbol that things were going smoothly and that my epilepsy had taken a backseat, leaving me in control of the wheel.

I decided to walk home with my friends on such a gorgeous day. As Karen, Rochelle and I skipped through the leaves and swung from the branches of the shortcut we took home every day, we just enjoyed being young. I waved goodbye as we parted and I began craving the Halloween candy left over from the week before. As I entered the house the warmth hit my face and my rosy complexion reflected the crispness of the day. I made a beeline for the cupboard and grabbed a box of chocolate-covered raisins just as the phone started ringing. Picking it up I was happy to hear another friend, Caren Anderson, on the other end. I had hardly spoken to her all day and was eager to hear all her news. As I munched on the chocolate-covered raisins, Caren filled me in on the latest soccer player crush she had and, in an instant, everything changed. The room felt fat—a feeling all too familiar to me. I couldn't move. Raisins spilled all over the floor, the phone crashed to the ground and only one thought ran through my mind, "Must lie down."

Forgetting all about Caren, I somehow managed to make my way to my bedroom in the basement. I lay on the bed with the room spinning, my legs numb, my arms tingling and the urge to urinate was so strong it somehow gave me strength to move my legs and attempt to stand. Each limb felt like it weighed a hundred pounds as I pulled myself into a standing position. Just as I got to a point where I felt comfortable, I fell forward and my face collided with a wooden door. I grabbed the doorknob in hope of softening my fall as my paralyzed legs sank to the floor. With my arms, I dragged my body to the bathroom, next to my bedroom, where I eventually passed out.

I woke up in my bed with Caren standing above me calling my name, "Cara, Cara! Are you okay? Can you hear me?" Confused at how I managed to get myself back into my bed or how Caren, as tiny as she was, carried me there, I tried to find the words to respond. My tongue was thick and my attempt to speak sounded like I had a mouth full of marbles.

"Wow, girl. You really scared me!" Caren exclaimed. "All I heard were the raisins falling on the ground and then the phone and then no answer. I knew something was wrong; my heart is still pounding." I just lay there, watching her speak to me, unable to respond. Closing my eyes, I fell into a deep sleep.

# CHAPTER ELEVEN

# DESPERATE DESPAIR

I woke up to the smell of dinner. I lay in bed for a while thinking about what had just happened, despair taking over my soul. The seriousness of the situation hit me hard. Not only were my seizures back, but the realization that I could have been driving a car the exact moment I fell to the ground made my stomach sick. What if I had killed somebody? I can't believe I was so stupid to think I could live a normal life. I knew it was too good to be true.

Standing up, I made my way to the washroom and I stood in front of the mirror for a long time, staring at my reflection. The anger and frustration bubbled beneath my skin like hot lava on the verge of eruption. My fists were clenched and my arms trembled. All I wanted was to release the pain, to make it all end. Like a creature had possessed my body, I had no control. I began punching myself and with every lash I felt calmer. I sank to the floor in tears, embarrassed and confused by my consistent need to release this way. Was I crazy? Why did I feel like this? I calmed myself, dried my eyes and pulled my sleeves over my arms to hide the horrible self-infliction. It was just one more thing I had to keep secret from the outside world.

At the top of the stairs, my mother gave me a big hug. She didn't have to say anything because her empathy was so apparent in her body language. "Honey, are you okay?" she asked with concern in her voice. "I was here minutes after Caren called me, but you were out like a light, so I just let you sleep it off. I am so sorry, sweetheart . . . I am so sorry."

My father got up from the table, wrapped his arms around me, and said, "We are just so relieved that you are okay, honey." His arms, like tree trunks, embraced me with loving confirmation.

"Thanks, guys. I'm pretty upset," I told them as I stuffed some of the hot supper into my starving body. "I could have killed someone driving in that car. I'm never getting my license . . . ever."

"Honey, I know that it seems that way, but never say never," Mom said with relentless optimism.

"Easy for you to say; you're not the one who just slammed her face on her bedroom door, almost pissing her pants and possibly killing someone with a huge metal machine called a car." Sarcasm seemed to become part of my permanent teenage personality and it did not sit well with either of my parents, especially my father.

"Cara," he said sternly from across the table, "I'm sorry you had a seizure, but that gives you no excuse to mouth off to your mother like that. Apologize to her right now."

I already felt sorry as soon as the words escaped my mouth and I saw the look of disappointment on my mother's face. As my cheeks flushed, my eyes stayed focused on the mashed potatoes sitting before me. I forced out, "Sorry, Mom," and felt hot tears streaming down my cheeks. Everyone at the table was silent. My brother asked to be excused and my mother and father inched their chairs closer to mine.

The three of us had been doing this dance for years now. In and out of hospitals, my parents watching their daughter lose the use of her legs, her memory shattered, hoping that every morning she would wake up. I spent years sleeping in a twin bed next to them so they could hear my breathing if something were to go wrong. Teachers challenged my parents' persistence in keeping me in the regular classes with my peers, knowing I would have a better quality of life, even if I struggled to keep up most days.

They knew it was all taking a toll on my self confidence, but I knew that it was also raping my parents' youth. I felt such guilt all the time. What would life be like for them if they had just adopted a normal baby? I thought about my birth mother and wondered what she would do if she was in their situation. Would she be as patient with my outbursts and the constant instability of my health? Who knows? All I knew was that no matter what my parents kept telling me, they loved me. I just wished I felt I deserved their love.

CHAPTER TWELVE

# THE IMPORTANCE
# OF SELF-LOVE

June 30, 2004

Dear Cole,

Almost 20 years later as I sit here in my family's home thinking of those days, it seems like a lifetime ago. I want you to know something I have learned without a doubt. My parents really did love me and they worked extremely hard to keep me here and, because of that, I have the extraordinary gift of being able to tell you this story. I understand now that my condition, my circumstance, really distorted how I viewed myself back then. Being beaten down, from life handing you struggle, often gets the better of people. I'm not even guaranteeing that you won't experience this yourself. I just hope that, from all that I have learned, I can impress upon you the importance of self-love. In the face of struggle and challenge, it can be an essential key to freeing yourself and raising you above whatever obstacles you encounter. In the end, it comes down to choice and how you choose to take what life hands you, my sweet little boy. Like the old saying goes, "When life hands you lemons, you make lemonade." You may not be able to control the situation, but you can always control how you feel about it. Always remember that.

Cara Jones

July 3, 2004

Dear Cole,

Everyone knows about my pregnancy now and most people are happy for me while others seem awkward. You must understand that my generation is much more open than my parents', as your generation will probably be more open than mine. Being a single parent is still often looked down upon by people in this small, Catholic town.

The thing that gets me, though, is that the mother still gets "tsked," but what about the dad who never decides to take his responsibility serious? I didn't crawl up on top of myself and get myself pregnant. I did get a little bitter towards men last week, but I reminded myself that not all men choose the wrong way. There are incredible men out there, like my Dad. He would never abandon us no matter how challenging it was raising two kids with special needs. I admire him for that and I know that he will be a great role model for you.

If you are a boy, as I suspect, I hope that I can raise you to see that women are special and deserve to be respected. People often don't know how to react to a situation like mine, but, really, they should look at the strength and courage the woman possesses in going through this journey alone. My hope is that someday they will.

I have had a series of ups and downs lately. I guess it's just a lot of adjustments. I feel like so much is changing in my life that I'm just barely holding on as I wait for the ride to slow down. I know God has given me absolutely everything I have ever wanted, including signs of His presence; I'm just so overwhelmed and scared sometimes.

I know you are going to be the best thing that has ever happened to me, but, right now, I feel emotionally exhausted. I need to feel the magic again! It is in my life every day; I just need to feel it. Sometimes I feel guilty even having thoughts like this when God has been so good to me. Here I am, 26 years old, and I thought I wouldn't make it this far. Like I said before, my confidence with my illness had gotten the better of me, but, sometimes when you least expect it, great things come out of difficult situations. I almost gave up back when I was sixteen, so tired of pretending I was okay, but then a man entered my life and things changed drastically. When I have moments like this, I think of him and I am reminded of how truly lucky I am to be alive and to be experiencing life.

CHAPTER THIRTEEN

# DR. DESTINY

I adjusted to life with seizures again after almost getting my driver's license when I was sixteen. I started looking on the bright side of things and talking to God on a more consistent basis. I wasn't sure why, but I was so connected to angels at the time, feeling their presence on many occasions. I surrounded myself with pictures of the mystical beings and devoured books pertaining to them. I began writing letters to God, telling Him all the things that were bothering me and asking him to please give me the strength to deal with my seizures and, in exchange, I promised I would do great things in the world.

Each time I finished writing a letter, I read it aloud to myself, reconfirming all that I desired for my future. Sitting on my knees, I folded my hands in prayer position, the temple of my forehead touching my fingers. Squeezing my eyes closed tightly, I focused on a crisp, clear picture in my mind's eye. I could see it, feel it and smell it—my life without epilepsy.

Now that I was 16 years old, I had to leave the IWK hospital and switch to a neurosurgeon at the Queen Elizabeth II Health Sciences Centre (QEII) up the road. My father took the day off work and he escorted my mother and me to our monthly visit to Halifax. We were all fairly excited and a bit apprehensive about meeting my new physician, Dr. Mark Sadler. Our experience, thus far, had not been very promising, and my previous doctor was not on my mother's favourite-person list.

It all began when I was about eight years old. I went into a series of seizures after being traumatized by a dog chasing after me on my bike. I had so many convulsions that I lost all feeling in my legs and was taken by ambulance to the IWK. For over a week, my doctor coaxed me up and down the hallways, determined to cure me of what they thought was a self-created affliction. I was only a child in their eyes, but I was no fool and I knew what they were thinking. They thought I was a fake.

After a series of tests my doctor spoke with my mother, privately, in his office.

"Mrs. Jones, there appears to be nothing wrong with your daughter beyond the fact that she seeks attention from her overly concerned parents." He sat behind his desk so self assured that my mother fought all urges to reach over and slap the judgmental look off his face.

"Excuse me?" Mom questioned, still getting over the shock of the statement as it hung in the air.

The doctor continued, "After all the tests, your daughter seems perfectly fine and my advice is to take her home and put her back on her bicycle."

Anger consumed my mother. She stood up in silence then turned to face the doctor.

"I'm not sure how someone in your position could even remotely consider that my daughter is a fake. You should be ashamed of yourself and see it as a failure on your part that you couldn't help her, but, as God is my witness, I sure as hell will find someone who can."

As we entered the QEII, all three of us blindly walked the halls in search of more than an office. We were searching for HOPE.

## CHAPTER FOURTEEN

# THE ANGEL OF VALIDITY

Dr. Sadler looked up at us with his gentle smile. "Well, Cara and Coleen, I have to say that it is very rare to find someone who truly has epilepsy, but, Cara, you are definitely one of them." He inched his way closer to us, his body language empathetic yet nurturing and professional.

"After reviewing the results of your EEG, it showed that your brain waves consistently reflected abnormal activity," he continued. "I would like to try you on several different types of medications to find the right one. If, for some reason, we can't find something to assist your quality of life, then I will recommend you for brain surgery. No matter what, I will help you as much as I possibly can."

My mother and I sat there silent, in shock. Who was this man? Where had he been my whole life? After all those years of being treated as a fake, having doctors look down on my mother and me with their judgment, this man believed us! His validation was like a warm breeze sweeping over my fragile emotional state. Staring at each other, my mother and I spoke without words, each of us saving face, our two different experiences united. We shed tears of utter relief. The future finally looked bright.

# CHAPTER FIFTEEN

# LIFE IS A HIGHWAY

July 7, 2004

Dear Cole,

Well, Cole, I'm sure you can see from that part of the story why I admire that man so much. He was the first person to look at me without judgment-just pure compassion. I felt so inspired by his genuine kindness and, when I think of him, I work harder to help others like he helped me. As I said before, not all men are bad, and it's men like him who make me feel great about bringing you into this world.

I'm finding it challenging sharing some of this information. You often hear people say they want to write a book but, when it's about your life, reliving these events can be quite daunting on the brain. It's good for me. It helps me put things in better perspective before you arrive. I do think it's important that I tell you about my experiences because there are many lessons to be learned from my mistakes, as well as my successes. As I told you before, loving yourself is invaluable. I used to truly hate myself. If I could go back as an adult and visit my child self, I would just hug that little girl and let her know that she is adorable. It is my only regret in life that I spent so many years loathing my own existence. I do forgive myself though and I understand that there were factors at work that were out of my control. I would say my hatred began early, but it was shortly after my medication therapy when the real devil sat on my shoulder.

## Drugs from Hell

The next few months, after meeting Dr. Sadler, were filled with highs and lows as I took the new medications. The first one, Frissium, I referred to as the drug from hell. Within weeks of it hitting my system, my personality began to change. I felt dark, alone and my self-loathing was at an all-time high.

There was one night in particular when I realize I needed to come off the drug. It was a Parish Centre dance, something we all looked forward to every month. At home, the phone rang off the hook, my girlfriends calling me trying to co-ordinate outfits and gossiping about who was going to hit on whom at the dance. So much of me loved dances and I was finally old enough to get permission to attend. Going to these dances was a symbol of adolescence and freedom. Our parents trusted us to do what was right, and it was a huge test, on their part, as well as ours. Everyone in town knew that half the kids went there loaded out of their minds. You could almost picture all the parents sitting at home waiting for curfew, praying that their kids weren't stupid enough to be one of them. There was not much to do in a small town and, eager to grow up, alcohol became the false language of maturity between us. Each week it became a shared goal: how would we get liquor? The whisper through the grapevine would eventually find someone who had an older brother or sister who was willing to take on the task of supplying booze for us minors.

I chose not to take part in the world of mind-altering substances. The drugs pumping through my veins were mind altering enough. The night of the dance, I picked out an outfit that I hoped would turn the heads of some of the clueless boys on whom I had a crush. I was taller than most the girls in my class, had long, black, wavy hair, and was thin with curves that seemed to appear overnight. I looked at myself in the mirror and prayed to God to please let them see me. More than anything I wanted a boyfriend. I watched all my friends dating boys and I watched the boys fawn over them. They made it look so easy. How come it wasn't happening to me? Although I wanted it more than anything, I was petrified. Every time a guy remotely looked in my direction, I froze and looked the other way. My shyness gave the outside world the impression that I was a snob and I became known as "the tall, black-haired one who hung out with Caren and them." There was only one boy whom I felt like I could talk to and that was Billy, my best friend, Rochelle's, boyfriend. He saw my true, fun-loving personality that I hid to the outside male population. One night I was riding around with Billy in his car, something we all did often. We laughed and carried on in hysterics at each other's ridiculous senses of humor when Billy suddenly spotted his friend, Peter, driving by. After catching up to his car, we pulled up, side by side, and Billy rolled down his window.

"Hey, Pete! What's up?" Billy asked in his typical easy-going nature. "Not too much, man. Just crusin' around, gettin' a bite to eat," Peter responded, looking into the car, smiling at me. I went silent and sunk into the seat, looking out the opposite side of the car. I was experiencing mixed emotions in that moment. Part of me was so proud to be with Billy and I wore his friendship like a badge that said, "See, I'm cool. Billy likes me." The other part felt petrified, paralyzed, and socially awkward. I lost all ability to speak. Billy looked over at me, waiting for me to take part in the conversation, but, simultaneously, they both picked up on my uncomfortable body language. "Well, see you later, man. Have a good night." Billy's tone was almost apologetic. "Yep, see you later, guys," Pete shouted back and with a courteous nod he rolled up his window to the cold night air and drove away.

Billy and I drove in silence for a few minutes, and he turned to me abruptly and said, "What the hell was that? Why are you so different around other people? It's like you are terrified!" Wanting the conversation to be over, I responded with a dry, "I know. Can you take me home now?" As we approached my driveway, I thanked Billy for the night and he said, "No problem, any time," with a soft, sympathetic look in his eyes like he was desperately trying to figure me out. All I could think was, "Good luck with that one."

Walking up my driveway, I mulled over my own fear. Billy couldn't quite understand. I mean, he was my friend, but what if he was dating someone like me and it happened? The inevitable, I could just picture it, my worst nightmare. There I am making out with my future boyfriend and BAM, I'm in a tonic clonic seizure with my body thrashing around, my face distorted and gasping for air, purple, drool seeping out the side of my mouth and gnawing on my tongue. Then, if they are really lucky, they get to see the finale of my epileptic dance, the "piss-de-résistance," my loss of bladder control. Yep, date me, boys, cause one thing is for sure, you'll never be bored.

So there I was, ready for the dance and even if I couldn't get a date at least I prayed for a slow dance. I loved the thought of being held in the arms of a guy, him looking at me, so completely into me. There was no denying it, I was a hopeless romantic.

I heard Mable (the car) pull into the driveway, bid my farewells to my parents and out the door I flew. In the back of the car, Rochelle and Karen pulled out a bottle of lemon gin. "You know what they say about lemon gin, girls?" Karen said "It's a sure panty remover." We burst out laughing and Karen cracked the screw-top bottle. Truthfully, we all knew that most of us were pretty inexperienced, or so I wanted to think. I guessed that Sadie and Rochelle went all the way only because they were in the longest lasting relationships, but I wasn't totally sure. The most I had experienced was making out with a guy that was three years older than me who told me he loved me after only knowing me a week. I might have been desperate for experience, but I knew a red flag when I saw one: a nineteen-year-old dude wanting to date a sixteen year old? Something just didn't seem right to me.

Once we reached St. Ninian's church parking lot, we piled out of the car and ran briskly for cover in the nearest bush. We never considered that if we walked we would look less guilty. Passing around the lemon gin, each of us commented on how good it tasted, trying to convince ourselves that the taste resembled nothing like Mr. Clean. The thought of mixing the liquor with anything like Sprite or juice never occurred to us because we knew that, if we drank it straight, it would get us twisted faster and we were aware that we had to be drunk by seven o'clock and sober by ten in order to make curfew. Of course, I was yet to see that ever happen and it became a game of how sober we could make ourselves appear to our parents.

I usually didn't drink, but I was feeling pretty down and the thought of forgetting the dark emotions that stirred inside me was too tempting to pass up. After indulging with my friends, we ventured down the hill to the dance.

As we drew near, we could see throngs of teenagers outside, littering the stairway, and we recognized some of our friends waiting to enter. You could hear the familiar sounds, coming from inside, of Tom Cochrane belting out his soulful cries about how "life is a highway," followed by C&C Music Factory's "Gonna Make You Sweat."

The last part of the test was sneaking by Kevin Pelly, the bouncer who was known as the man you never want to make eye contact with, especially when you're guilty. If he got one glimpse of your glossy pupils, it was straight to the next room where the RCMP set up shop, handing out $365 fines as lessons for underage drinking. If you could walk a straight line past him, pay for admission and get your hand stamped, it was home free from there. Luckily the alcohol hadn't quite hit us yet and we were in the clear as we strutted down the dingy stairs and headed to the bathroom to fix our hair.

The fluorescent lights in the bathroom kick-started my buzz and, before I knew it, my face was flushed and I had a rush of liquid confidence. I made my way to the dance floor, ripping it up with the girls and having a great time.

As the music began to wind down, I recognized the next tune and my heart sank to the floor. Madonna, in her deep, sensual voice, sang "Crazy for You," and I watched my girlfriends stumble toward their boyfriends. I stood there alone, having to take the long walk to the sidelines and watch as they swayed back and forth, groping and fondling.

So much of me loved that song and so much of me hated it. All I wanted was to be asked to dance to a slow song; it didn't really seem like that much to ask. Why did they all look through me? I felt like I was invisible in the eyes of men and I hated it. Who was I kidding, I hated myself. I no longer wanted to be at the dance and the dark cloud that had been hanging over my head now seeped into my soul. Instead of dancing with a cute boy, I got stuck dancing with the devil on my shoulder who insisted on whispering everything but sweetness in my ear. In that moment, my cocktail of epilepsy drugs from hell and lemon gin induced a depression, causing me to feel like I wanted to die. Despair became my new companion and I knew that something had to change or I would succumb to its temptation.

# CHAPTER SIXTEEN

# LEMONS VS. LEMONADE

July 10, 2004

Dear Cole,

Since I've been pregnant, I've had so many ups and downs. I think a lot of it has to do with adjusting to life standing still. I've been moving for years now and when I wasn't moving I was planning my next move. Sometimes I'm excited about you arriving, but sometimes I find it so hard to believe that I am actually pregnant. Maybe it's because I'm not really showing yet or I need to start reading more to make it feel real. All I know is I'm sick of feeling like an emotional roller coaster. I guess all of these hormones I'm producing do not really help. I think if I buy one of those books I found on Amazon for single mothers it might help. When I read books about pregnancy I can't relate because they are geared towards couples. Even the books on single parents don't feel real enough. I want to hear somebody's story. I guess it will all come together sooner or later; I just have to be patient.

I know I sound pessimistic. This is not really my style! It's so weird having all these emotions; I'm usually so much lighter than this—grateful and loving in the moment. I guess I have to appreciate that this is not really in my control sometimes, that I do actually live in a human body that makes me act and feel things I would rather not. I remember feeling this way before and I made it through that experience; I'm sure I can handle this. I just need to breathe.

## **Butterfly Girls**

The summer I started the new medications became a haze of highs and lows. I decided to grow my hair long and to take pride in my appearance in hopes that it would mask the inner tug of war the drugs played on my self-esteem.

One morning, in early August, I decided that my eleventh year in school would be different. I wanted to change and no longer wanted to be the shy, dark-haired, nameless girl who hung out with so-and-so. I wanted people, especially boys, to know me.

The first week of school, I consciously stood taller, looked people in the eye and flipped my long hair as an indication for boys to pay attention. That weekend, the girls and I were invited to a party at a university student's house. I saw this as my opportunity to somehow get noticed, so I did what worked best in our age group, I drank.

The funny thing is I did feel the alcohol, but not so much as I pretended to. I wanted to be aware of what I was saying, but knew how everyone would think if I just started talking out loud after years of being silent. "Who the hell is this girl and why is she talking now?"

I had a plan, so I began implementing it about an hour into the party. I knew what guys wanted: an "in" to all the girls I had access to daily. There were three guys sitting on the sofa, Shane Delorey, Dan Quinn and Brian Clifton. I had been going to school with these guys for two years now; Shane even had his locker underneath mine for our grade-nine year. I spoke to him only a handful of times the entire time, petrified he would see the enormous crush I had on him. I felt pathetic because I blushed with every word I spoke when confronted with a male presence. For some reason, the alcohol erased that condition and I used it as my window to start a conversation.

"So, who do you guys like?" I blurted, surprising them with my spontaneous question.

They looked at each other, taken off guard by not only the question but the fact that I actually had a voice.

"I don't know," each chimed in simultaneously, laughing at each other's synchronicity.

"Oh, come on, guys, give me a break. I know you like someone. Tell me who they are!" I urged.

"Why do you want to know?" Brian asked suspiciously.

"Because," I informed them, "they are all my friends and I can help you get to know them." I trailed off. "That's if you want me to." I knew full well they did.

So my plan to shed my high school reputation of the invisible nobody had now commenced and they bit it—hook, line and sinker. By the following week, I was using the three-way-calling option on my phone to hook people up. I would call the guys, which gave them an excuse to get to know me, and then I would secretly call my girlfriends, with the boys silently listening to hear if their crushes felt the same way. I only did it once before I let the girl in on what I had done and soon I became the middle person who sparked new relationships all during our eleventh grade. It was much easier talking on the phone with your crush, if she or he knew there was a middle person taking the pressure off. I became cupid and soon my popularity increased.

This new-found status took my mind off my medical reality and helped me form relationships with guys to whom I had never spoken. Even though I was the "friend" and not the "girlfriend," I prayed that one of them would see how great I was and sooner or later ask me out.

That day arrived sooner than I expected. Shane Delorey and I began calling each other on a daily basis. We would talk for hours about every facet of our teenage existence. He was the first guy to call me who didn't have a girlfriend and I knew he liked me. I waited patiently for him to get the courage to ask me out.

A few months went by and we girls were preparing for a big party happening in town. We decided to make electric Jell-O at Rochelle's house, something none of us had tried before, but looked forward to the creation process. Rochelle had purchased Christmas tree Jell-O moulds at the local grocery store and we mixed the ingredients together with the quart of vodka our friend's brother had secured for us. After letting it chill, we dug into the green mass of delicious intoxication, waiting for something to happen, and happen it did. I think it was the first time we had tasted alcohol that it actually tasted good and our gluttonous selves took over. We ended up wasted and I laughed like I hadn't laughed in a long time.

Arms linked, staggering down the street, trying to walk straight at any sign of oncoming traffic, we walked up the shortcut to the party at the top of the hill. The brisk winter air felt amazing and I remember, in that moment, feeling like this was one of the best nights of my life!

As we entered the doorway, we came face to face with hundreds of teenage bodies jammed together, laughing and talking over the music. I saw Shane in the corner and our eyes met with the joint reaction of pleasure in seeing each other. I knew something was going to happen that night. The evening progressed and my connection to Shane grew stronger as the night went on.

"Wanna go for a walk outside?" he finally asked.

"Sure!" I answered so nervous I thought I was going to get sick right there, but knew that might not be the most attractive thing in this moment.

We walked into the backyard toward the barn that sat just off to the side of the house. Our feet crunched in the snow, breaking the silence of our teenage awkwardness. Upon arriving at our destination, I leaned up against the green, paint-chipped shingles and, as I did this, Shane leaned in towards me and we began kissing as if it were the last time we would kiss. The sexual tension had built up over the weeks and it felt good to release it finally in this moment. I didn't want it to end and felt the power and chemical surge of being desired by a boy. He was the second person I'd ever kissed, but this time, it was different—I was different.

About ten minutes into our make-out session, we started getting cold and, not being very experienced, we had no problem in cutting it short. My friends greeted me around the corner with looks of excitement they tried so desperately to contain so not to embarrass me, and we all made our way down the hill back to Rochelle's house.

The second I walked in the door, the girls were on me, screaming with joy over my triumph. They sang, danced and teased that I finally got my turn and I would be lying if I denied that it didn't feel good.

Shane and I continued dating for a few weeks but, in the end, we both felt we were good friends. This whole experience put me on the available list for guys and they started to take notice of me in social situations. This alone assisted me in camouflaging the negative self-talk that bounced around the shadows of my inner world. I went on to do well in school that year, in comparison to others. By that summer, I had a close-knit group of girl and guy friends who embodied the support I had always dreamed of. What I had manifested was one of my first lessons in proving that a proactive mind in a state of turmoil can rise above most circumstance.

In July, I got a call from Dr. Sadler that became the catalyst in the transformation of my life with epilepsy. I would be admitted to the

Victoria General Hospital in Halifax and undergo weekly observation while hooked up to an EEG machine, tracking my brain waves. This was one of the pulmonary steps in determining my admission as a candidate for neurosurgery. I was extremely thrilled at the prospect of being chosen for this procedure and I didn't care what I had to do to be considered.

# CHAPTER SEVENTEEN

# RELENTLESS SUPPORT

July 15, 2004

Dear Cole,

Today I heard your heartbeat for the first time and it felt like I'd been given the gift of a miracle, but it wasn't until today that it felt real. Hearing that thumpity-thumpity-thumpity, I felt an excitement and love that I had never experienced before. Wow! I'm making a little person! This is so amazing!

### Poem by Cara

She wondered would time remove the sheets from their eyes
Stumbling with ignorance in the shadows of beauty
Wearing crosses like badges, pulling rank with their faith
Preaching God's disappointment in her with silence

Jesus stands by with His hands on her belly
A gift unconditionally loved lay inside
His head hangs, he sheds tears for their blindness
A vision of courage and strength in her choice

Wiping the moisture from His face, she smiles
Forgiving the judgment they placed on her life
Dancing the rhythm of two heartbeats in one
The onlookers squinting at their light, they skip out of sight

July 19, 2004

Dear Cole,

I had a great time the other night at the Concert Under the Stars. My friends laughed at how I just blurted my news. People would ask the regular question, "So what have you been up to? What are you doing now?" I would answer very matter of fact, "Well, I just traveled the world for three years and now I am going to have a baby." It may have been a little bit on the shocking side, but I know how this town operates—its' gossip central. I would rather they hear it from my mouth.

Sometimes I look at my friends and feel so grateful for their support; I have been lucky that way. I have always had girlfriends who were there for me.

Poor Rochelle, I remember the time she experienced me having a seizure while I spent a short stint in the hospital one winter. I think it was in that moment she understood the capacity of what I dealt with as a person with epilepsy and why I was always so scared of guys seeing me in that state.

Karen has been one of my best friends from the time I was thirteen years old. We have always been the two girls who hung out with the guys in our late teen years because we couldn't handle the drama that came with being friends with teenage women. Guys just told it like it was and we loved that. So Karen became my protector and always distracted people when she knew I was having a seizure. Most people, besides Rochelle, Karen and a few others, couldn't tell when I was having an attack because, after I turned 17, they changed and my tonic clonic seizures only happened in the night while I slept. Partial complex seizures were the ones that occupied my day and, by the summer of 1995, when I was being admitted to the hospital for the pulmonary EEG tests, I was having about 50 of them a day. It was while in the hospital that I understood the magnitude of my supporters and my undying determination to be "normal," whatever that meant.

# CHAPTER EIGHTEEN

# SUMMER OF SUBDURALS

I set out for the big city to check into "Hotel VG," better known as the Victoria General Hospital, not really knowing what to expect. As I greeted the staff upon arrival and became familiar with my surroundings, the nurses took me into a room where they glued the subdural wires onto my scalp. These would track my brain waves and record any seizures. I was instructed to push a button when I felt one coming on and immediately the machine would kick-start the documentation process.

I settled in quite comfortably, watched quite a bit of TV, read a few books and, when I felt a seizure coming on, I pressed the little button. The problem was (which I can't believe I actually described as a problem) my seizures stopped. I couldn't understand it; I usually had so many in a day it was ridiculous. I tried not to get too worked up about it even though I was concerned. I was there to be approved as a candidate, but who would approve someone who didn't have seizures.

Thankfully, a few days later, I got a great surprise when my friends, Karen, Cody and Brian, all showed up at my door with a big stuffed toy and some Kentucky Fried Chicken. I was so glad to see them. As a teenager, it's strange how your friends become your world and everything they do is so influencing. Their love for me was so strong that my lack of self-love became lessened. Sure, I had insecurities, and maybe it was just a maturity that began unfolding within me, but optimism was born in me during my seventeenth year and I never wanted to revert. No matter what medication haze slammed against me, I continually swam up above the wave, gasping for air and rejoicing in the sweet taste of breath. I could sense my purpose on the horizon and I believed that I was going to have what everyone else did—opportunity."

The next two weeks went by quickly, but the wait to find out the results of my observation felt like an eternity. As I waited, my health began to decline rapidly. Fifty seizures a day turned into over one hundred and, as I embarked on my graduate year in high school, my optimism was laced with unconditional fear. Something deep in my subconscious knew that, if I continued on this way, I would fall asleep an optimist and never wake up.

# CHAPTER NINETEEN

# LET GO AND LET GOD

July 30, 2004

Dear Cole,

I have been doing so much in the past couple of weeks that I actually feel as if I lost weight instead of putting it on. I've been going to the beach with my friends and I went mackerel fishing for the first time since I was a kid. I used to have no problem killing fish when I was younger but now, as an adult, I had a hard time with it.

Later that night I went to see a Slow Coaster concert—one of my favourite bands. I met a lot of people I hadn't seen in a while, including an old crush from high school. My girlfriend pointed him out and said "Wow, he is the marrying type for me!" I couldn't help but agree.

The thing is, there are moments when I'm out now and it will hit me. Everything that I know as normal is going to change. I feel like I can no longer see a guy and think, "Hmmm, maybe," and then go for it. Now I have to think, "Not a chance," and walk away. Even though it's a big change, I don't think it's a bad thing. I need to learn to say, "NO," and not fling myself into every wrong situation out there. Now I will let opportunities come to me. It's going to be weird, but worth it, in the long run, for both of us. I can't settle for just anyone!

Much of my anxiety is starting to leave now. Fear is something that is so futile, but we all experience it. I have felt it so many times, but I think I've experienced situations above and beyond this one that make this fear seem like a phobia of thunderstorms. It's loud, bright and makes itself know, but the chances of it destroying me are slim. So, in other words, I am feeling much stronger. I keep praying every day for you to stay inside me and for God to continue to give me inner strength. So far, it's been good. The bigger I get, the more real it feels. I'm soon to have an ultrasound and I'm pretty excited!

## The Graduate of a life less ordinary

The fall of my graduate year, I felt pumped. Every single day I looked at the Nova Scotia College of Art and Design poster, closed my eyes tightly and begged God, "Please!"

The relationships I had with my friends grew stronger than ever, but I continued to hide the secret of how my struggle with seizures had tripled in number. The optimist continued to do situps in my subconscious and each day my mind grew stronger. "Never say never" became tattooed in my consciousness. I studied, I read, I wrote, I drew, and then, I had seizures and forgot it all. I continued this pattern every day and smiled at everyone in the process. My artistic self began to show through in the conformity of a small-town high school where different meant exclusion. I wasn't quite sure how to let that part of me out without ridicule because, even though I didn't want it to be true, I cared what people thought of me.

Then one day the call came, the call that would change everything. Dr. Sadler told my mother that I had been accepted to undergo the neurosurgery and, within a few months, I could be in London, Ontario, being prepped for this life-changing event. Mom, Dad and I sat at the kitchen table after Mom hung up the phone. The energy in the air was hard to ignore.

"Well, this is it! This is the moment we have been waiting for, guys," my mother finally piped up, breaking the strange moment of silence we all shared. "Guess it's time to start planning."

She headed down the hall towards her room to do what she did best—organize.

I still sat there not really sure how I was feeling. I truthfully couldn't believe it. After all this time, all the seizures, all the pretending I was okay in moments when I really wasn't, my prayers were finally answered. I noticed Dad looking over at me and he noticed the tears that began gathering at the corners of my eyes.

"What's wrong, honey," he asked, soothingly, as he inched closer to me, putting his arm around my shoulder.

Not really sure what to tell him or how to explain the emotions I was having in that moment, I did my best.

"I am so grateful," my voice broke up and I continued on, "and I am scared, relieved and excited all at the same time." I looked up into my father's empathetic eyes and wondered in that moment how he was feeling. Here I was sitting in front of him, the teenage daughter who he watched grow up. The daughter he fought for and worked hard for so that she could have the best quality of life he could provide. He loved me, nurtured me, watched me slip away from him on more than one occasion and, with his strong, callused hands, he pulled me back each time with his unwavering love. I never told him often enough that I was always in complete awe of him. Even in those moments when we didn't see eye to eye, he always had the purest intentions of love. Sometimes I would ask God for a partner like him some day, one who would look at his children like he did at Chris and me, someone to give our children like he selflessly gave to us. He is my hero.

"It's okay," he said as he squeezed my shoulder into him. "We will take this on together like we always do."

In that moment, I let the gratitude flow through me, and all other feelings that accompanied it. It was a defining moment where I sat at the gateway to infinite possibility and the key to what awaited me on the other side arrived in all its glory.

# CHAPTER TWENTY

# FIGHT OR FLIGHT

August 01, 2004

Dear Cole,

Tonight I'm having severe cramps. I sure hope I didn't strain myself working too hard. I find I'm having horrible sleeps and my memory is such that I feel as if I am losing my mind, especially at work. It's so embarrassing!

Cole, I really hope you are healthy and make it to full term. Even though I fantasize sometimes about the old life I am letting go of, I want you to enter my life. I just need to start taking better care of myself, physically, by improving my nutrition and spirituality. I find work is exhausting me, mentally. In moments like this, I remind myself of where I have been and how lucky I am. It feels like it wasn't that long ago when I prayed to God to give me the chance to live, and now I am here and I am not only living, I am creating life.

## The Aerodynamics of Life

The months, between getting the phone call about the surgery and actually driving to Halifax to depart on our flight to London, passed like a blink in time. As our car travelled along the highway, trees danced along my view, bare branches sprinkled with snow. I couldn't help but think of the many metaphors for seasons and change—how in that moment all that I had experienced was now being stripped away and exposed like the trees in winter with the knowing that, in just a few months, I would be experiencing growth and blooming like the promise of spring.

This was my second time on an airplane, but, I had to admit, it looked much different through the eyes of an eighteen year old. It had been four years earlier when I flew to Fredericton, New Brunswick, to visit my friend, Laura. I remember the flight attendant placing a huge, red, circular sticker on my chest with the word "Minor" in big bold letters, announcing to the staff that I was traveling alone. Most teens would have been mortified by the embarrassing symbol, but it really didn't faze me. I was just so happy to get the chance to go away on my own.

Now, at eighteen, pushing my trolley down the hallway, I was more aware of the magic that an airport possessed: people reuniting, students leaving home, and business people high from their newest deal. Faces, tears, laughter, feet shuffling—these were all sounds of transition and I found it beautiful and exciting.

"I find these places so darn confusing!" my mother piped in, breaking my observational bliss. I could sense her stress level; she wasn't very good at hiding it, although she was convinced she was.

"I mean, where the heck is the gate? I don't understand a thing these signs are telling us."

I smirked and found Mom's total lack of direction amusing. It was something I definitely must have inherited from my birth parents because my sense of direction is flawless. I could find my way out of a maze blindfolded.

"No problem, Mom. Just follow me," I said as I quickly guided her through the bustling hallway towards our gate.

"How do you do that?" My Mom asked, in awe of my ability.

"Just a knack, I guess," I responded, finding the simplicity of the situation welcomed, considering what lay ahead for us both.

As passengers began lining up, my mom and I stood face to face in silence. My mother had never been on a plane before and here she was about to take flight on a journey whose outcome was uncertain—smooth and steady or rough and filled with turbulent undertones. I grabbed her hand to comfort her and gently let her know that I was pretty confident about the whole ordeal.

Once on board, the flight attendants began preparing for takeoff, stowing luggage in the overhead compartments, placing chairs in an upright position. I watched as my mother's eyes became like a child's, following every move with wonder. Soon the seatbelt lights were on and we began taxiing down the runway.

"Relax, Mom," I whispered gently noticing her white knuckles grasping the arm of the chair, sheer panic painted on her face. Once we were in the air for about twenty minutes, colour finally returned to her cheeks.

"Whew, that was intense," she slowly exhaled.

Knowing that Mom was finally relaxing, I decided to pull out my book and I reached down into my bag, eager to escape into its mystical contents. As I pulled it from the bag, the image of an angel's wing came into view and the woman sitting next to me perked up with interest at the sight of it.

"A fan of angels, I see," she commented, inching a little bit closer to me.

"Yes," I responded, eager to share my passion with anyone who would listen. "I know they are around me; I can feel them on an ongoing basis."

"You know, it's quite rare to see someone as young as you into such a spiritual topic," the woman said, looking at me with great intrigue.

"Yes, my belief in angels has definitely helped me through some difficult times, that's for sure," I replied with testimony in my voice.

The woman's eyes looked into me and, for a second, I blushed bashfully at the thought of her viewing the parts of my soul I kept hidden.

"I'd love to hear about it, if you don't mind sharing. My name is Alice," she said as her arm extended to embrace my experience kindly.

For the next hour, I shared my story: the hardships, the rewards, and the gray in between spots along the way. When the plane started to descend, Alice spoke to Mom and me with conviction in her voice and stressed how brave we were.

"God is watching over you both." She nodded then gave us both a hug. When Mom and I got off the plane, we both felt the same way, but it was my mother who voiced it first. "Looks to me like we just met an earth angel." She squeezed my hand and gave me a wink.

## The Ward

When we arrived at the hospital, Mom and I were escorted to the epilepsy ward. As I entered the doors, I observed the large room that housed ten beds, five lined up against either wall. The floors were carpeted in a cozy brown tone and in the middle of the large room was a small nursing station. For a hospital ward, it actually felt comfortable.

I was happy to get a bed with no one on either side of me and tried to settle into my new home. Mom, who was staying at a convent, left shortly after to adjust herself to her new environment. About an hour later, a young girl came up to my bed and introduced herself.

"Hi, I'm Angela," she said as she shook my hand and took a seat on the end of my bed. Angela and I hit it off right away. There was such a genuine kindness about her and I was struck by her natural beauty. Her eyes were big and brown with green flecks and she wore her brown hair short which really emphasized this feature. I could tell after only a few moments that she had been through a tremendous ordeal for such a young person.

This was Angela's second time going in for brain surgery to correct her condition. She was 19 years old at the time and she told me how life was for her in high school, living on serious doses of meds that made her lose all her hair. People used to call her names like "dyke" or "les" and my heart broke for her. She went on to tell me that the surgery only worked for a short time and, while she was studying to become a nurse, the epilepsy came back in full force.

"All I ever wanted to be was a nurse," she continued her eyes reaching out to me, longing for an empathetic friend. Like a dancer with a shattered knee and forced to retire, Angela was told her dream would never happen. It was not possible for a nurse who went into convulsions to attend a patient. I had just met her, but I reached out and grabbed her hand. I knew what it was like to be told "never."

I don't understand why people go that route when dealing with others who face adversity. Why didn't they tell Angela about all the other areas of medicine she could pursue? Instead, they told her she couldn't be a nurse. I vowed that if I ever got to the point where I became an authority figure, I would do my best to help people find "something" they could call their own, instead of constantly handing them "nothing."

Angela didn't have many friends. I couldn't understand why because she had such an amazing personality that captured you the second she opened her mouth. I soon realized that many of the older patients felt the same way and that my life had been blessed in more ways than I could comprehend.

A week after I had settled into the hospital, my grandmother, Dorothy, gave me the gift of television and phone connection at my bedside. Elation was an understatement when Mom gave me this news. I had read all the books I had brought with me and had played about as much Scrabble with mom that I could handle. This definitely wasn't my first long stint in the hospital as a teenager. I had been in and out of the hospital every year of my life until 16 when I got a year-long break.

Once my phone was connected, my friends started calling non-stop. One day Angela and I were playing checkers when the phone rang.

"Do you have this every day?" she asked in a far away voice.

"What?" I responded, thinking she meant the phone connection, but soon realized it was deeper than that.

"Friends," she replied under her breath as she moved her black circle to a square. I sat there in that moment with the epiphany of how lucky I was to have this life, the friends, and the support I cherished. I never fully appreciated it until this moment. I wanted to take her pain away, but knew I couldn't. All I could do was be a friend to her now, so I smiled. Almost as if she knew what I was saying without words, she smiled back.

# CHAPTER TWENTY-ONE

# TRANSITIONAL SQUALL

August 6, 2004

Dear Cole,

Every day I become more comfortable with my body changes and my future as a mother. I guess sometimes these things take time to adjust to and, considering my life has drastically changed, I know it is all for the best. It is time for my life to drastically change.

I am starting to understand the worry that mothers have for their children and find myself praying that I can give this baby the best life possible. It's frightening sometimes to watch the news and see all the scary people out there whom you never want your child to meet. I've made so many mistakes and I hope to protect you from that also.

I hope I can teach you to love yourself, to feel self-empowerment and know that you have control over your destiny. I had so many people in my life tell me "never," but I proved them all wrong. I want you, my baby, to know that "never" is a state of mind that "CAN" be changed.

## <u>Pain for Pleasure</u>

The first day I arrived in the London hospital, they glued subdurals to my head, wires glued to my scull, to run a constant electroencephalograph (EEG), tracking my brain waves to pin point the exact location of where my seizures were coming from. The only problem was that it was stress that triggered my seizures and I had none of that here. Boys, friends, and school—they were all gone. I was just sitting around watching TV and playing checkers. It was the longest I had gone in years without a seizure and, I have to say, it was the first time I ever prayed to God to actually make me have one. If they couldn't track the location, it meant I was going to have to have subdural surgery and I definitely wasn't looking forward to that.

Subdural surgery entailed drilling holes in my scull and laying the wires on my brain in order to give them an even more accurate reading. So, like I said, I was praying for a seizure and soon.

Having the subdurals constantly connected to a machine meant I could never take them off and, even when I went to the bathroom, I had to take the wires with me. Bathing became interesting, and privacy was something I had to sacrifice, short term, to achieve the quality of life I dreamed of.

Sometimes at night I felt energies around me, things I knew were there, but I couldn't see. I knew it was my angels. I could feel my future. They were helping me feel it and I wanted to believe them, but I was really scared. What if I didn't make it out alive? What if this was it for me? Over and over, whenever I felt this fear, a warm breeze would wash over me, like they were telling me to have faith. Faith was the one thing that kept me going so I tried to listen.

Week three came with no sign of seizures. The doctors finally made the call to give me the subdural surgery. Every Monday, my neurologist and all the interns would flock around my bed. They would discuss me, never using my name, and I always wondered if they got tired of pretending I was a person without emotions. I knew it was to protect their emotions, but sometimes it frustrated me. I wanted to scream out to the young interns, "Do you have any idea how scared I am?" but I knew it was no use. Everyone needs protection, especially them. I couldn't imagine what it was like to go from patient to patient seeing that much pain without protecting oneself. Despite this, I loved my nurses and doctors; they were always so sweet to me. That is why I felt so badly for them the night I begged them to kill me.

It was the day of my subdural surgery and they told me when I woke up I would feel some pain because, although there are no nerves on the brain, my skull would be irritated and there could be swelling. Irritated! They made it sound like a mosquito bite.

My mother walked beside my bed as they wheeled it down the hallway, reassuring me that it was all going to be okay. I was so scared. What if I felt it? As they took me into the sterile room, I got a glimpse of the tools on the side of the table. "Oh, God, please give me strength!" I prayed, intensely, over and over in my head.

"Okay, Cara, we are going to give you a little gas to relax you and then we will give you a needle that will put you to sleep. Are you ready?"

"*NO,*" my mind screamed out. "Yes," my voice replied.

The mask went up to my nose and I looked up at the ceiling. *"Please, God, don't let me feel anything. Please, God, don't let me feel anything!"* I repeated over and over in my head.

"Okay, Cara." The doctor spoke so softly, as if soothing the inner child he could see peering through my eyes.

"When you feel a pinch I want you to count backwards from ten," he instructed as I listened to the motion of busy hands preparing for the procedure.

PINCH.

I felt a warm feeling in my arm and run through my body. "Ten . . . nine . . ." Soon I felt heavy and all that was left was my subconsious. Again I felt the presence of energies and I knew they were angels. They lovingly looked at me with invisible eyes and I was taken away by them, amazed at their love for me. They consoled me telepathically, reminding my soul that I had chosen this. It was all coming to fruition and, although my physical self did not understand what was happening, my spiritual self confirmed what the angels were telling me and, for what felt like a brief moment, I bathed in the bliss of this knowledge. Then SLAM!

For the second time I was faced with the unbearable pain of living in a physical shell. I didn't want to open my eyes. I wanted to ignore the nurses who were calling out my name. I didn't want to be here anymore, feel the pain anymore. I wanted to be with those loving beings who made me feel so good, so filled with knowledge.

I knew the angels were right; I knew I had chosen this. I just wish I could remember why. My eyes slowly peeled open and I was back in the ward. My face felt funny, my head pulsated and my stomach churned. I couldn't respond and, even if I could, I didn't want to. I leaned over the bed and vomited. Unimaginable pain pierced my skull with the pressure of my heaving. The nurses quickly scurried for a bucket to catch my bile and they rubbed my back in the hopes of comforting me.

It was the middle of the night and my mother had been called back to her dorm by the nuns. She was told if she wanted a single room the only way she could get it was if she returned immediately and made her bed. Mom explained to the nuns that I was in surgery and, if she left, I might wake up, but they were strict with their rules so she left, hoping I wouldn't wake up while she was gone.

I was glad my mother wasn't there. I didn't want her to see me like this and, in my delirious state, I knew it was my only window of opportunity to ask the nurses to do what I needed them to do.

It had been three hours of vomiting. I couldn't take it anymore; the pain was just too unbearable. Each time I felt that familiar feeling rising in my stomach, up my esophagus and out my mouth, I braced myself: sharp torture, knives scraping, pressure gripping, pain.

I mustered up enough energy to finally plead, "Kill me," I whispered.

"What?" the nurse leaned in, probably denying she heard me correctly.

"Kill me!" I begged this time. "Give me a shot, please! My mother will understand; she wouldn't want me in this much pain." Completing the request, I vomited more bile.

"Honey, you know that isn't right," one of the nurses replied tenderly. "You need to live, sweetheart. The world needs you. Your Mom and Dad need you."

All I could think was *"Kill me! The pain is too much! Kill me!"*

Those nurses never gave up. They loved me, and comforted me as the pain coursed through my body. Their words of encouragement became the lifeline I needed to survive. For the rest of my life, I will remember their kindness and how the smallest act of love can evoke the strongest act of healing.

I finally fell asleep and awoke the next day with my mother stroking my hand.

"You did it, Cara. You made it through; you're going to be fine." I was happy to hear my mother's voice and glad in that moment that the nurses didn't listen to my pleas. The pain was still the worst I had ever experienced and, when I caught a glimpse of myself in the mirror, I could barely recognize the image staring back. My face was swollen and my eyes sunk into the puffy mass, unable to stay open. So I closed them in hopes that the pain would be forgotten in unconsciousness.

Over the next week, my face started to resemble something more recognizable, but the pain continued. I ate as much Benadryl as they would allow because it usually knocked me out cold. One day, I overheard the nurses asking my mother if I usually slept this much outside of the hospital.

I knew they were concerned but, at the same time, I found it a strange question, considering what my head had just been through. Once the pain started to subside, the itching became unbearable. It felt as if there were a thousand ants crawling on the inside of my head, yet there was no way to relieve it. I tried to tell myself that after this experience I would never complain of a headache again.

My friends were a great release from my daily routine of eat, sleep, bathe and sleep. One day, I was on the phone with my friend, Brain Clifton, who was always cracking jokes to try and lighten my mood. The problem was he was so ridiculously funny that every time I spoke to him and laughed the pressure on my skull was too much to handle. Thank God I could take it in small doses and remember his crazy sense of humour during the rest of the day; it always managed to put a smile on my face.

All of my friends were preparing for the semi-formal dance and I was disappointed that I was going to miss the last semi-formal with my graduating class, but it was a small sacrifice in the long run. My friends were really the solid rocks in my turbulent high school experience and they reminded me of this with their constant support. I got a great surprise one night when they called me from our friend, Laura's, house as they got ready and waited for their dates to arrive. Each of them got on the phone and reminded me how much they loved and missed me. It was fun hearing all the excitement and their silly, slurred, alcohol-induced speech they tried to cover up unsuccessfully.

After hanging up the phone, I sat on my bed for a while then attempted to get up and walk to the washroom. I made my way up to the sink and leaned on it, still a bit weak after all these days. Looking back at me was my swollen face, but behind that face were young eyes. I spoke out loud to my angels in that moment, making a vow that I was determined to keep.

"I know you are here," I said softly, breaking the silence of the room. "I know you are listening. I promise I will work hard to get out of here and live my life. I promise never to take this experience for granted. Please help me get out of here in one piece, preferably a highly functional piece."

I stared into my eyes a little longer, took a drink of water, then made my way back to my bed. I wanted to go home now. I wanted to restart my life. I prayed that I got the chance.

# CHAPTER TWENTY-TWO

# RESERVOIR DOGS

For three weeks prior to subdural surgery I prayed that I would finally have a seizure. My prayers were answered and small seizures started occurring. Each time they did, I had to press a button on the side of my bed which would record my brain waves. With this information, the doctors would be able to locate the exact spot on my brain where the seizures originated.

One day, my doctor told me that I was ready to go for surgery in just a few days. He left behind a documentary on the surgery so that I would know what was ahead of me. My mother put the video in and was completely glued to the screen, but I just turned my head away and begged her to turn it off. Was she crazy? I didn't want to see what they were going to do to me nor did I want to hear about it. If it was anything like the horror of subdural surgery, I would rather not know.

The next day, Todd, the boy across from me, was preparing for his journey to the operating room. He found out that he was going to be awake during the process and he was doing his best not to freak out; I could see it in his eyes. They kept reassuring that he wouldn't feel a thing, that the brain does not have any nerve endings, and that he would be frozen so he wouldn't be uncomfortable. As I listened in on this conversation, I became weak, closed my eyes and prayed over and over, *"Please, God, let me be asleep. Please, God, let me be asleep."*

I wasn't sure if I would be able to handle the thought of being awake. Memories of the many times in the dentist chair flashed through my mind. The dentist reassured my mother that I was just seeking attention when I said it hurt so much, only to find out years later that they had been drilling and I was never frozen. My mouth didn't handle freezing in the normal way. Instead of believing me, the dentist did what I had experienced time and time again, she ignored my pleas. What if this experience was the same? What if, while I'm lying as they saw open my skull, I can't speak to tell them I can feel every bit of it? I closed my eyes tightly and tried hard to get the image out of my mind. I began thinking of summertime and the beach. Soon my nerves settled, for the time being.

While Todd was getting his surgery, I sat in fear. Hours passed and I tried to occupy myself with television, reading, walking, anything to take my mind off what he might be going through. Finally, he was escorted back onto our ward, groggy, but alive. I felt a weight lift off me, not really sure what I was expecting, but, after all, it is our brains they are messing with here.

The next day, Todd could speak and, when I asked him what it was like, he said exactly what I feared, "Horrible."

He went on to tell me the details of being conscious of what was going on, but not feeling anything, only being mentally uncomfortable of the fact that his brain was exposed and he knew they were probing at it.

"Oh, dear God!" I cried out. I thought, "I need to get the hell out of here!"

The room felt smaller, my heart pounded and I looked at every possible escape, but I knew I was stuck. I had to go through with it; I prayed I was going to be asleep.

Sure enough, the next morning, the doctors showed up and surrounded my bed. They asked the usual questions. "How are you feeling? How is your progress?" Then, as casually as if to ask me where I was going on vacation, the doctor asked how I was feeling about being awake for the surgery.

"AWAKE!" I exploded, "What do you mean, awake? Nobody told me I was going to be awake!" He looked at me perplexed.

He continued, "Well, yes, you are going to be awake, but don't worry, you won't feel a thing." With that they left me alone as they moved on to the next patient.

I stared at the floor. I wanted my mother. She was out having some time to herself, but I desperately wanted her here. Maybe she would let me leave. I could live with the seizures; it wouldn't be that bad . . . right? Panic began to take over and I decided to go and find my surgeon.

I made a beeline for the elevator, in total denial of what they told me. *"I can't do it!" I thought. "I don't have it in me to be awake; this can't be right!"*

My surgeon's door was open and he was surprised to see me when I appeared in the entrance way.

"Cara, how are you? What can I do for you?" I loved his calm voice; it made me feel at ease in this moment of sheer internal horror.

"I can't do it," I began, "I can't be awake! There are a lot of things I can do, doctor, but this is not one of them. I will feel it; I know it. I will never be the same again. I don't want the surgery. I want to leave. Please, please let me go," I said in one continuous breath. The doctor sat back, alarmed.

"Cara, take a deep breath. It's going to be okay," he said as he went over to the water cooler to pour me a glass of water, seeing that I was panting at this point. "I'm not sure who told you this, but you are not going to be awake, sweetheart."

His words were like cold water soothing my feverish flesh.

"What?" I responded. "The doctors upstairs said . . ."

He immediately interrupted, "Well, I'll find out who exactly those doctors are, but they were very wrong to tell you this when it's completely false."

He sat back down and looked satisfied at relieving my anxiety.

"Cara, I will tell you, in my honest opinion, even if you had to be awake, I know you could have done it. I've seen you over the past couple of months and I know what you are capable of. This would have been no different."

Although flattering, to some degree, I seriously didn't care about how strong he deemed my character, I was just so thankful I was going to be asleep. I walked out of his office and headed straight for the chapel across the hall. As I knelt down, I felt an invisible presence beside me and again I knew I wasn't alone.

"Thank you," I whispered. "I will never forget this."

A warm wave encompassed my body, affirming my sense of not being alone and I smiled at the confirmation.

# CHAPTER TWENTY-THREE

# THE WARRIOR INSIDE

August 9, 2004

Dear Cole,

If you are a boy (which I believe you are), I want you to know how precious women are. They have a built-in strength to overcome adversity for the love of their children. I also want you to know that you can be whatever you set your mind to.

If you are a girl (which I am pretty sure you're not), I want you to understand you have the right to achieve any dream you set your mind to, that your heart is a special prize to be won by only the most worthy and that your body is a temple that you should cherish. If someone were to come along and try to violate it, your spirit will be strong and you can overcome anything. Respect is what I want my baby to learn, whether you are a boy or girl. Learn to respect others, as well as yourself.


September 1, 2004

Dear Cole,

My summer continues to be amazing with beaches and dancing—a summer I will never forget. Living with Mom and Dad is okay, but sometimes I feel I might go crazy with Mom's over protection. I know I should be grateful and, truthfully, I am, but sometimes it's hard to push away her fear when she smothers me with it. Most women don't have the support I do.

I am the lucky one and I try to remind myself of this with every incident that arises between us.

I haven't had much money lately with student loans and such, so she offered to pay for my long-overdue haircut. I gave the hairdresser a three-dollar tip, which I usually did, but it sent my mother into an absolute frenzy. It was the breaking point for her and she began hollering at me in the car.

"How could you tip three dollars when you don't have three dollars?"

In my mind, it was just a normal thing to do—when you get a haircut, you always tip your hairdresser.

"I'm sorry," I said. "I will pay you the three dollars back." The point is, it was never about the three dollars. She knew I had no idea what I was getting myself into and the only way she knew how to communicate was to raise her voice loudly!

"How are you going to provide for this child? How are you going to feed it, Cara?"

She kept hollering and I tried to stay calm, but, the louder she got, the dizzier I became.

"Stop it, Mom, please!" I held onto the door handle, ready to jump. She didn't stop. I finally lost it and started hitting the door, screaming at the top of my lungs, "LET ME OUT! LET ME OUT! LET ME OUT!"

I finally got her attention and she stopped, urging me to calm down. Ha . . . calm down? I'm 26, living in a one-horse town, pregnant with no father for the baby, and living with my parents who have no idea that I am actually an adult! I sure didn't feel like an adult in that moment. It's interesting how your parents push certain buttons and, out of the blue, your child self emerges which they can easily blame. It's an exhausting battle in which I feel I am screaming into the wind.

The worst part about that whole situation, besides the part where I felt like I might be losing my mind, was that I was scheduled to have my first ultrasound in an hour and I was so worked up I didn't want to go. Thank God I got over it because, when I went into the ultrasound, it was the most amazing thing I have ever experienced. There you were, my baby, so healthy looking and moving around.

So far everything looks good and I couldn't be happier. I couldn't believe how detailed the image was—I could see your arms, your legs and your face. I feel so much closer to the life growing inside of me. God, I hope I'm a good mom.

I find my hormones the most challenging part of the pregnancy and I am glad that is the case. So many people have such difficult pregnancies; I'm so lucky. Sometimes my emotions are wild, I cry at the drop of a hat and feel frustrated and insecure, more than I have ever felt. I'm so conscious of myself being single in this town that I'm even shocked by my own insecurities. Previously I was the women's rights advocate, the warrior, the goddess, not some woman who feels shame at what other people think of her.

Not too long ago, maybe a couple of weeks, a few friends of mine went with me up to the city just to walk around and window-shop. As soon as I arrived, I felt like I was breathing in freedom, like this was home. There was a sense of anonymity about the city that I loved. Blending in, nobody knowing my business—it was wonderful! I know I don't want you to grow up in Antigonish, but I get so scared about moving out on my own, especially if I'm going to be going to school. I hope I can find the strength and patience to do it. I so badly want to find the warrior inside me. She's in there somewhere.

I am grateful for all the people in my life: they want to love and help me so much. I understand my Mother's fear. After all we have been through together; she only wants the best for me. I can't even imagine what it's like for her to see me in this situation after all she has endured trying to give me life.

## A Poem by Cara

*Some days the warrior hides*
*In these moments of untrained*
*Life*
*Idle eyes all of a sudden*
*Matter*
*The feminist voice is lost*
*In a whirlwind of hormones*
*Two heart beats under the skin*
*Of an artist gone*
*Colour blind*
*She pulls out her sword*
*Tangled it with memories*
*Fighting back against herself*

# CHAPTER TWENTY-FOUR

# PERSISTENCE

The week after finding out I would be awake during my surgery, I was prepared to undergo the procedure. Every single day I thanked God for coming through for me on this wish and I felt I could take on this journey a lot easier. Again, I went through the formalities of no food beforehand, the doctors talking me through all the stages of what I could expect and, the next thing I knew, I was being wheeled down the hall towards the unknown. I was so scared, but I felt that familiar invisible presence moving along the corridor with me and then I heard a voice from inside me which was not my own.

"It's going to be fine, Cara."

I felt calm and knew whomever was with me had my best interests in mind.

The doctor brought the mask up to my face, instructing me to count backwards and, as I felt myself slipping away, I heard the voice again and for a moment I recognized who it was.

**Blackness.**

I became aware again of the entity standing over me in the darkness. I knew that he was someone or something that I have been close with my whole life. My mind felt free, as if someone were lifting me out of my body and cradling me in warm love. As he rocked me back and forth, I experienced information being poured into me, an understanding of why this was all happening. Then, with child-like excitement, I remembered who he was.

"Dini!" I said, as I relaxed into his loving arms, trying to see something. Confirming my discovery, I felt his pleasing aura change and, as we reunited, Dini continued to speak to me energetically. I understood everything he told me and was overwhelmed with the possibility of it all. I could feel myself slipping back into my body and I resisted with every ounce of will power I could muster—to no avail.

What seemed like only a moment was actually sixteen hours and my eyes opened to the feeling of intense pain. My limbs were heavy as lead and my head, a detached piece of meat that somehow housed my thought—all memory of that moment with Dini now replaced with unimaginable torment. I could hear my mother's voice so desperate to soothe her daughter's excruciating discomfort.

"Hi, Cara," she said softly, trying to reach me, but my spirit fought the urge to rejoin this lumpy skin shell. Soon I was able to respond with a very weak, "Hi," and then drifted back to sleep.

This time there was no vomiting and I was so unbelievably grateful, but the magnitude of the pain was too much to bear, let alone find the words to express it to my mother or the doctors.

"Look, Cara, the package from your friends arrived," Mom said, gesturing to the end of the bed, hoping to cheer me up. I lay there realizing that something is different. I felt calm in the midst of chaos. Although I had no strength to leave my bed, strength was building from the inside out. I knew I was getting the hell out of there.

Over the next couple of days, I worked tirelessly to get my strength back. I started with walking to the washroom and back, then sitting up in bed for short periods of time. I was in the recovery centre, a few floors down from my regular ward, but I noticed, one day as I ventured to the doorway, that the hallways were somewhat quieter than I would have expected. I made a commitment to myself that I would walk those hallways to build my strength and that I would be out of that hospital and on my way home in a week. I shared this goal with my doctors.

"That is a nice goal, Cara," they responded with doubt, "but we have never had anyone leave that soon after undergoing neurosurgery."

I just looked at them and replied, "Well, there is a first time for everything!"

I played the soundtrack of Reservoir Dogs over and over as I walked up and down the hallway, holding onto the railing for support. I willed my body to heal and, after three days, even my mother noticed an incredible difference in my recovery.

On the fourth day, the doctors came in to take my bandages off and clean my incisions. I was nervous, but relieved, when they told me that it wasn't going to hurt and that the area around the incision would probably be numb forever. They left my bandages off so the air could help me heal. It felt good to feel the air again.

As I looked in the mirror, I reminded myself of something out of a horror movie: a scar and staples right up the middle of my skull, running down the side of my head to my ear, blue and bruised, but a symbol in my mind of gruelling transformation—the beginning.

I quickly grabbed my earphones and made my way to the hall. I could see the amused look in the doctors' eyes; they respected my drive, but doubted the speedy results. Two days, later they were in my room for the last time to remove my staples and prepare the paperwork for my discharge the next day.

My doctor looked up at me from the paperwork, paused for a moment, then laughed at the knowing look on my face.

"Well, Cara, you did it! You definitely proved us all wrong. Did you know that you are the first person in our hospital ever to recover from brain surgery this quickly?"

"No," I responded, feeling proud to be the first.

"It says a lot about your determination and I hope that you use that same drive in every situation with which you are faced."

I said, "Well, all I can say is, I will try."

The next day my mother and I said goodbye to all our friends and the doctors and nurses who helped me on my journey. Nurses, who brought me back from the "dark side" the night I begged them to kill me, hugged me extra long and I whispered a quiet, "Thank you."

As they wheeled my chair to the exit, I watched the patients in their rooms move past my vision and I prayed to God in that moment. "Please, God, let this be for real! Please let me live!"

The staff opened the doors to the outside. The sun shone brightly, I squinted and embraced the warmth that awaited me on the other side, and moved forward towards unimaginative possibility.

# CHAPTER TWENTY-FIVE

# THE ART OF CHANGE

September 2, 2004

Dear Cole,

It's been challenging these past couple of weeks. I feel as if I'm always defending myself. People always seem to have something to say to me about being a single mother. Honestly, I really don't feel it is any of their business.

Then I come home and Mom pushes her fears about my pregnancy onto me. I just don't need it. I am my own worst critic. I am the one who thinks about it the most! I wish everyone else would just keep their opinions to themselves.

I finally sent the letter to Jason's mother yesterday. I'm concerned she won't write back and, then again, I'm scared she won't be the person I hope she is. I do forgive Jason for being an idiot, even though some days are easier than others. At least I am getting the gift of you, my wonderful baby. I feel sorry for Jason. He won't get to know the little person he helped create. Maybe someday he will come around. I just hope he doesn't decide to write me after his mother gets the note and it's nasty. I'm going to have to be strong for that. A few of my friends, and I, sent Reiki to the letter. I hope it helps in finding its way to her. I feel she has a right to know her grandchild. I really hope she is a good person and I did the right thing, but my heart tells me that I have. I will leave it in God's care. Until then, I will work harder to feel better about myself. I am a strong person and I want you to know that. I want to love you and give you the best life possible.

Later: You have been moving all day; it's a nice assurance. I'm going to try hard to switch this crap in my mind to positive for the both of us. Sorry, baby!

September 5, 2004

Dear Cole,

Things have been looking up the past couple of days. I feel like there is a cloud that has lifted from my eyes. You are constantly moving now and it's such a crazy, great feeling. I have my ultrasound appointment with the doctor this week to go over the results. I hope everything is okay, but I'm sure it will be.

The other night, when I came home from work, I saw that my friend, Sara, a friend I met in Korea, sent me a great postcard from Montreal to cheer me up and to tell me how happy she is for me. It was so sweet, and definitely worked! I just love her so much.

Yesterday, I prayed to God before I went to work to help me have a better day, and I did. A woman also came into work and I met her eight-month-old baby! It dawned on me that I had never seen an eight month old and, when I looked at her, I realized there was no way I was going to send my baby to day care that young. I felt so much better, relieved almost. I guess I just need to take it one day at a time.

**From Sara:**

**Horray! I know postcards can cheer people up, but it's even nicer when they arrive just when they're needed! I can totally sympathize with the raging hormones and everyone says it does go away after awhile.**

**I definitely think you should pursue your dream of going back to school, but, if it is to be postponed, that's not the same as abandoning it. Eight months old wouldn't be too young for you to go back IF you had a full-time—stay-at-home partner but, other than that, it would really be hard. You'd have to leave the baby with a babysitter at such a vulnerable time. But you'd be surprised at how much help there is nowadays for moms who want to go to school. I think people realize that one major reason women are still lagging way behind men in pay equity and in post-secondary education is that when a girl and a guy conceive a child, the guy can go on with his life and the girl is left with all the physical and financial burden AND the resulting human being who takes 15 to 20 years to grow up and become independent! But times have really changed. I**

know that at McGill there is free child care for all student parents and there are even volunteer babysitters who go to your place if you need to get away to study or even if you just want some company. Plus, there's the Student/Parent Network where all students who have kids can get together and compare notes, share stuff like car seats and toys, and trade babysitting favours with each other. Concordia is usually way more progressive than McGill, so keep checking out the school idea and you may be able to do it sooner than you think. If you come to Montreal, you can sign me up for free babysitting relief! We lived with Issaac in Korea, from six months to over a year old, and have lots of experience with diapers, feeding, etc. Plus, I was a nanny for three summers for a little guy who was two years old when I started. Cara, it just hit me! You are going to have a kindergarten baby of your VERY OWN! Nobody understands the "Korean Kindergarten Baby" feeling like you do (I still look at their pictures and cry). I remember all those times we said, "I wish I could just take them home with me . . ." You got your wish☺

Cara, please don't stop making art! Even though I was crazy busy last semester and over the summer, I MADE myself stop to draw or paint a few times, just to remind myself there are other aspects of me other than studying. I even ended up with a couple of little paintings I really like. (They are really amateur, compared to my Nova Scotia College of Art and Design friends . . . painting isn't my strong point; but it felt good to make something and like it!)

I have to run but hang in there with the hormones.

Love, Sara

September 7, 2004

Dear Cole,

Writing this journal to you has been so challenging and rewarding. I'm sure it is not unlike parenthood. Art is something that is very important to me, but sometimes I feel I have come face to face with a true identity crisis. How do I continue to be who I am and be the mother I need to be for you? I am sure it will all come together; life always has a way of working out. I have already learned a lot at such a young age and, although others may think I am crazy, I am grateful for these experiences, no matter how challenging they appear.

Returning home from the hospital with my whole life ahead of me, I naively thought the healing process would be easy. That summer proved to be one filled with turmoil and lessons that I carried with me for years, but, by the grace of God and all the help of those who love me, I found the light like I always do. I hope that when you are older you pick an easier route, but, if you choose the hard way, I will be there to help pick you up like so many have done for me. You need to trust in the Universe, Cole, and all will fall into place as it should.

# CHAPTER TWENTY-SIX

# THE YING AND YANG

When I returned home, I was so excited to see my friends I could barely contain myself. I knew I was about ten pounds lighter and I tried to sport my bandanna, which covered my whole head, with confidence. I didn't care. I just wanted to be a teen again and experience my graduating year with my friends.

Dad had picked us up at the airport and wrapped his arms tightly around me, so glad that his little girl was okay. I can't even imagine how torturous it must have been to be so far away from Mom and me, with no idea of what I was going through, only what Mom could share with him over the phone. He was such a strong light in my life and, being back in his arms again, was confirmation that God had given me another chance to live. I wouldn't let either Him or my Dad down.

As we pulled into the driveway, my best friend, Karen, was waiting for me. She squealed as she ran towards my door, ready to pull me out and hug me tightly. "Oh, my God, I am so glad to see you," she exclaimed as her arms extended to take me in an everlasting embrace.

"Come on up stairs and see all the gifts people brought for you," she announced, leading me up the stairs to our back door.

Balloons and flowers decorated the whole table in the kitchen. Friends and relatives all shared their joy over my arrival, making my heart completely swell with gratitude.

My brother, Chris, came up the stairs, happy to see me, and also gave me a warm hug. "Did you bring me anything?" he smirked, his usual question every time we returned from being away. Of course, I always knew it meant, "I missed you."

After we ate, Karen told me that all our friends were at a hockey game and, knowing I couldn't handle my excitement to see them, Mom agreed to let me go. She thought I was crazy to go to a hockey game so soon after brain surgery, but she knew that, after the ordeal I had just gone through, seeing my friends was therapeutic for me. So Karen and I hopped in the car with Dad and off we went.

I had only been away a short time, but everything in town looked different, smelt different, felt different. I was different. I understood as I watched the houses go by that life was never going to be the same again because that was exactly it. It was life. I had life.

We thanked Dad for the drive and I told him I could be picked up in an hour. The smell of the arena hit me instantly and I knew I was home. I walked into the packed rink and saw the look on all the faces aware of my presence. Almost as if you could hear the scratch of a record, signifying the awkwardness of the moment, all conversation, all music and all activity stopped and people stared. I didn't care; I expected it and I found my way over to my friends. Their joy in seeing I was okay was painted widely across their faces. We sat and enjoyed each other's company. They asked me questions and I happily answered them, discreetly, giving only the positive view of the situation. I just didn't feel it was necessary to expose them to something they didn't need to know, as if I were trying to prolong their innocence with my smile and careful words. I was just so happy to be back.

An hour passed faster than I had hoped, but I was more than ready to go home and shower in my own bathroom without anyone knocking on the door every two minutes. Don't even get me started on the thought of sleeping in my own bed; it was going to be amazing.

I waved goodbye to my friends as I hopped back into dad's car and drove down the streets of my small Nova Scotian town. It seemed brighter than I remembered, even in the cold darkness of the evening.

After returning home, I was quick to bid good night to my parents and make my way down to the basement. It felt like yesterday when I begged them to let me live downstairs so I could have my independence. One flight of stairs can seem like a mile for parents who were never sure if I would wake up in the morning. Now I was back from a life-altering experience and my independence grew into a broader reality.

My head hit the pillow and, as I started drifting to sleep, I looked forward to the day when I was completely healed and that the strange, crunching sound of my skull fusing back together was no longer my lullaby.

I returned back to school pretty quickly and enjoyed being among my peers again. It was only a few months before we would all be graduating and I couldn't wait to walk across the stage with my friends and celebrate our future endeavors together.

The reality of my situation really hit home for my peers when, a few days after my return, we were hanging out and my friend, Murray, asked if he could see my head. I continued to cover it up with a bandanna, but indulged in the request and showed them what lie underneath. I watched the expressions on their faces change from curiosity, to horror, to amazement.

"Holy shit!" Murray exclaimed, breaking the silence in the room. "I mean really. Holy shit!"

We all just looked at each other and began to laugh. The scars on my head were huge and they started from the front of my head, straight up the middle and down the side to just above my ear. The indents of the staples and the black ointment looked like train tracks along my skull. Murray and my four friends surrounded me to get a closer look.

"I know you were sick and went away to have brain surgery, but for some reason it never seemed real until now," Murray continued as he viewed the medical miracle.

Over the next couple of weeks, as I got into the swing of school again, I received the nickname Chia Pet because my hair was growing straight up and out of my bandanna. Things started to look great and I felt lightness in my step, but, after about three weeks, the lightness began to feel a little heavier. It was almost as if the high of my situation was over and a low started to replace it. I became extremely exhausted and those old feelings of self-loathing started to creep in.

My best friend, Karen, had shaved her head a couple of weeks after mine was shaved and, although she said it was to support me, I wished she hadn't done it. I hated that I didn't have any hair. I felt so unattractive and now, with her hair gone, we looked like a lesbian couple. I had no issues with people being lesbians, but the attention I was getting in a small-minded town was not something I particularity wanted. One day, as I walked down the street, a couple of young guys hollered, "dyke!" and threw a pop can at me! Strangely enough, even though it was hurtful, I was glad to have the experience because it made me sensitive to the pain that so many gay people face—not only gay people, but people who are victims of bigotry and other forms of abuse. Hatred is so senseless.

One night, at a party, a guy who was a few years older than me, kept looking me up and down with disgust. Finally, after a few more beers, he came over to me with his cocky energy flying all over the place.

"What are you trying to prove anyway?" he said. His comment threw me off guard because I didn't know him and I was such a sensitive-hearted person. The last thing I was trying to do was prove something.

"I'm sorry," I said kindly, "but do I know you?"

"No, you don't," he snapped at me. "It just pisses me off that people like you go around flaunting themselves. Why would you shave your head? You look terrible and, trust me, we get your message loud and clear!"

I heard every word this guy said to me, but his hatred seemed so irrational that it conjured calmness in my demeanour and all I could do was stare at him.

"You know," I responded with a sincere feeling of sadness for his ignorance, "you shouldn't be so quick to judge people. You might find out that there is more to their story than you can see on the surface."

"Don't tell me what to do," he continued. "What do I need to know other than that you are a dyke and that you don't belong here?"

I stared at him again, my silence and lack of response making him fidgety and uncomfortable.

"Yes, that is what you would think, isn't it? Well good luck with that." I walked out of the room and my friend, Laura, followed me. Everyone in the kitchen had witnessed the whole scene unfold and nobody said a word, as if they knew I had it under control.

"Are you okay?" Laura asked, while squeezing my arm, showing me comfort.

"Yeah, I'm fine, especially knowing I am much more sensitive than that jerk." We both smiled.

In the kitchen, my good friend, Garrett, looked at this guy with total anger and protectiveness for me.

"What the hell is your problem, man?" he asked him, giving his arm a little shove. "Are you out of your mind or something?"

"Why do you say that?" he responded, feeling good about expressing his opinion and disapproval of me.

Garrett quickly filled him in. "That girl just went through hell and back; she just had brain surgery, you dumb ass! That's why she doesn't have any hair."

The young man's face drained of colour that the six beers had given him, and he went completely silent. He walked quickly to the back room where I sat and I saw shame written all over his expression.

"Garrett just told me what happened! I am so sorry. I didn't know!"

I did give him credit for coming and apologizing, but I knew he had a lot to learn. I took the opportunity to let him know it.

"What if you didn't find that out about me?" I asked, gazing on him with questioning eyes. "Would you honestly treat someone that way because they were different than you?" I quickly took on the role of the mother scolding the child and noticed how his eyes lowered in response.

"I hope you remember this moment for the rest of your life and maybe the next time you are so quick to judge, you will think about it."

I walked past him and out the back door. I had just about enough of that scene. I said goodbye to my friends outside and walked down the street, feeling the refreshing air on my face. I smirked and couldn't help but laugh at his ignorance and how damn good I felt to have stood up for myself. I continued to laugh out loud as I ventured to my parents' house to call it a night.

# CHAPTER TWENTY-SEVEN

# IN GOD I TRUST

September 10, 2004

Dear Cole,

Well, baby, your mother is starting to feel back to herself again. It amazes me how much of a haze your mind can get into when someone is occupying your body. I guess a lot of it is just fear and feeling overwhelmed with the responsibility that lies ahead.

One day, if you are a female, you will experience this transition, physically and mentally. If you are a male, you will feel it emotionally (if I raised you right-wink), and you should be there for your partner because together the transition will be smoother.

I watch all these things on TV and I get so scared of how crazy the world can be and pray I have the knowledge to teach you how to protect yourself from the monsters who sometimes lurk around the corner. Everyone has so much faith in me that I will be a good mother; I hope I don't disappoint them or you! I give myself up to God and I just have to trust in the fact that I was given the gift of you for a reason. Together we will be a team and rise to any occasion.

There is so much I want to teach you and so much I know you have to learn on your own. One of those things is about God. Many people will give you different information on this subject and all I can say is that he exists. I know because I have seen Him; I have been there. There is another place and time that we've come from and I've always known this since I was a little girl, drowning from fluid in my lungs, thrashing around from a tonic clonic seizure, floating above my body as they tried to revive me. I told the doctors what I saw and what they said to each other as they worked on my body. I never forgot that or the gift of second sight that I received at that time. I've always had a knowing about things, baby, before they happen. I have always been given glimpses to reassure me. This gift has been in our family for a long time: your grandfather and Uncle Anthony also have it. I've always known it exists, and I have a feeling you will, too!

Many of these glimpses have occurred since conceiving you. Those moments are gifts in themselves. I am so grateful for this knowledge (even though, secretly, it scares me sometimes) and I cherish it.

Over the past couple of weeks much has happened. I sent the letter to your grandparents in Australia. If they received it, I'm not sure, but I did send it registered mail. I also found out that your father is on a rough path right now, but always remember that it has nothing to do with you. When I found out, I felt a sense of relief, I have to say. I could finally let him go, knowing that his path was not my fault. His ignoring me was deeper and he has a lot of healing to do before I can ever allow him in my life, and, especially yours.

Sometimes you just have to let it go. There is nothing I can do, so let it go. I did the same thing this week when my boss told me my shifts would be cut to two a week. At first, I was devastated, but then I just smiled and let it go! I trust in the Universe and know that these things are happening as part of some plan. I have to trust! We will both be alright. I promise that!

I have always had faith and it has proved to be my saving grace. Let me continue to tell you the story of how things got dark for me, but how light continued to shine beyond the shadows.

## Spirituality 1996

I worked really hard the next few months and, although I had no idea how long it would take me to get into NSCAD, I was really looking forward to graduating and getting out of high school. I thought I was in the clear, but soon I started to realize that something was terribly wrong. Hopelessness began creeping up on me. I wasn't exactly sure where it was coming from because I was feeling so grateful to be alive and, whenever the feelings would stop in for a visit, I would always feel guilty. I didn't have a right to be sad. God had given me a second chance at life and it was everything I ever wanted. So why did I suddenly feel so low?

My parents noticed the shift in me as well and, after they found me in my room one night, crying so hard that I broke all the blood vessels in my eyes, they knew whatever was happening wasn't normal. They called the doctor right away and were informed that one of the side effects of this type of surgery was mild depression. Mild depression! Now that was an understatement if I ever heard one. Anyone who breaks the blood vessels in her eyes from crying is definitely undergoing more than a mild depression.

Soon my grades started to slip and the teachers delivered the news that would top it all off. I was not going to graduate with my classmates. I did not take this news well; in fact, they might as well have delivered the news that I was dying of cancer, I was so devastated. I cried like a baby for hours in my room, so angry, and not understanding that after all this I still wasn't normal. I hid my sadness with a smile and became overly excited for my friends, taking part in all the graduation activities and jokingly saying that I was spiritually graduating.

I did love the new-found freedom of staying out late with my friends, watching the sun come up and our pre-grad parties as we sat around campfires on the beach, planning our prom dresses and our dates.

I might not be graduating, but I was at least going to love every second of that particular time in my life as much as I could. My friends wouldn't be together forever and, as we all hugged each other, drinking beer, and looking up at the stars, we all knew it, and held each other that much tighter.

The hype before graduation was a great distraction from all the doubt I was trying to ignore. Each morning I would stare in the mirror, willing my hair to grow in time for prom, even though I didn't have a date yet. When I did get one, I wanted to look good.

There were many magical times in those weeks and, although I was fighting a serious depression, I was still in awe of the beauty of each day. How lucky I was to have my friends and, although my future was unknown, at least I had a future to look forward to.

A few weeks before the prom, my friend, Greg, who had graduated the year before, heard I was looking for a date and asked to be my date. I was so happy and relieved to have someone as fun as Greg for my date. I loved his demeanor and humor. I knew, without a doubt, that we were going to have a great time.

The days leading up to the prom were filled with activities and my mother thought it would be a nice idea to have all the girls over the night of the church service at St. Francis Xavier University. It was known as one of those big moments, when everyone stands outside of the chapel and throws his/her hat into the hair, waving goodbye to childhood and welcoming new experiences. I knew I wasn't graduating, but I wanted to go and support all my friends who had worked so hard for this moment. My friend, Laura, ruled against my idea. She also had to be held back a year, but planned on getting her last three credits through a distance course.

"Don't do it, Cara," she warned. "You will only torture yourself!"

I didn't know what she was talking about. I wasn't torturing myself; I was supporting my friends who mean the world to me.

"You're crazy," I joked with her. "You should come with me."

"There is not a chance in hell I would set foot in that church," she exclaimed. "Girl, you're the crazy one."

I got all dressed up in my new red shirt and long, red-flowered skirt. I felt good and glad my hair was co-operating. I finally had the tiniest bangs, but they were bangs, and I was so happy to finally have them for prom.

I entered the church by myself and quickly found one of my friend's brother and sister-in-law who invited me to join them. I gratefully accepted and stood there, gazing at the sea of blue gowns and caps in front of me. I waved to my friends and they waved back. As I lowered my hand, the reality hit me. Laura was right. What the hell was I doing there? My expression quickly changed from optimistically proud to realistically devastated and anger began to flood my body. Like a raging beast caged inside me, my thoughts became wild and uncontrollable.

*"You deserve to be up there,"* my thoughts echoed. *"It's not fair. This is so ridiculously unfair!"*

As I listened to my thoughts like an innocent bystander, I couldn't have agreed more. Tears began gushing down my hot cheeks and I made my way down the aisle and out the door.

Holy crap, keeping up this positive outlook was challenging. I felt so happy for my friends, I wanted to be there for them but, in the end, this really sucked! What did all of this mean? Where was I supposed to go now? I sure as hell didn't want to go back to high school. Screw that nonsense—it just wasn't worth it.

I stood back and watched all the students in their blue gowns and caps leaving the university chapel and gathering to stand on the steps. On the count of three, they all threw their hands into the air for the photo opportunity for which they had waited four years.

As I observed the celebration from the sidelines, I was over my meltdown and I accepted my current situation. There was nothing I could do about it so I might as well embrace it and party with my friends.

Prom was only a few days away and I was super excited that my hair had grown back enough to actually look good.

I borrowed my friend, Carrie's, long, red, fitted dress that she had worn to the prom the year before and every night I tried it on and stared at myself in the mirror. My curvy hips and C cup breast fit the dress perfectly. I admired the reflection staring back and, for the first time that I could ever recall, I actually felt sexy. With that thought, I couldn't help but realize that somewhere along the way I had shed my girlish figure and miraculously transformed into a woman.

Greg picked me up and we began our night of dinner, drinks and dancing! Everyone looked amazing and it was exactly how I had always imagined the night to be. I was so happy!

At the dance, a slow song came on and Greg and I made our way to the dance floor. As we swayed back and forth, I couldn't help but reflect on a few years back, praying for someone to ask me to dance, and here I was.

I noticed this beautiful girl, Sara, a year ahead of me, dancing next to us with a guy that I had a crush on. I then noticed Greg staring over at her with that starry look in his eyes.

"What's the deal, Greg?" I asked with a huge smile that snapped him out of his love trance.

"Oh, nothing," he blushed.

"Come on," I said, nudging him. "I saw the way you just looked at her. Do you guys have a thing going on?"

Finally he started spilling, "Yeah, actually I really like her and I think she feels the same way about me!"

Greg was such a sweet guy, and I had absolutely no feelings for him beyond friendship so I was excited that his crush was dancing right next to us.

"Greg, I am so glad you are my date but, if you like Sara, what are you doing dancing with me?"

I could see that Greg was shocked by my question. "'Cause I am your date, Cara, and I'm having fun hanging out with you."

"I know, Greg," I said, squeezing his arm, "and I am having an amazing night, but this is your chance to make your move. Go dance with her and I will go catch up with my friends. I'm happy just being here . . . really!"

The joy that lit up on his face I will never forget. He hugged me so hard I almost lost my breath.

He spoke into my ear over the loud dance music, "Seriously, you have to be the coolest prom date ever!"

I smiled up at him and said, "I like to think so!" Then I pushed him away and said, "Go get her already, you fool!"

I skipped to the front of the floor where my friends were "shakin' their groove thang" and for the rest of the night I celebrated love, life and friendship. It was one of the best nights of my life!

# CHAPTER TWENTY-SEVEN

# SUMMER SABOTAGE

I developed a fear of school after being unable to graduate with my friends. What was the point of going back? I studied so hard only to walk into an exam, have seizures, forget everything, panic and feel stupid, and write on the bottom of the page to the teacher, "I'm sorry." It was more than I could bear to put up with anymore. I gave up.

Something started happening to me that spring which I couldn't understand. I constantly felt guilty about the fear and anger that consumed me, especially since God had given me a second chance. I cried all the time, continually breaking the blood vessels in my eyes. It looked like someone had punched me in both eye sockets and was difficult to explain to friends and family.

My mother became concerned and called Dr. Sadler to find out what she could do for me. He informed her that since the brain tumor was removed from my right temporal lobe, the part of the brain that controls emotions, I was susceptible to depression and probably would have to deal with that as a side effect for the rest of my life.

I had felt depression before, but nothing like this. It had become so debilitating that I almost wished for the epilepsy to return.

My friends and I usually hung out at our mutual friend, Leslie's, apartment. She was eighteen and had lived on her own for a couple of years. I found it a refuge during this time of transition and being around everyone who was experiencing a "normal" teenage existence was refreshing.

I was a virgin at that time. I had a few sexual experiences with some of the guys I was dating and one time, after a Legion dance, I came close.

My virginity was something that I never really cared much about; to me it was just another step of making out. This, no doubt, was a symptom of my low self-esteem and mind-altering drugs that polluted by body.

Most people I knew had gone all the way but, now that I had no hair, I was pretty sure I would be waiting a long time to experience that moment. I was wrong.

Another one of the side effects, I came to understand years later while in my twenties, was an increase in libido. Nobody ever explained that to me or my mother. Maybe they assumed I was too young and it would not be something I would have to deal with. They were wrong.

That summer became one of the pinnacle periods of self sabotage and it took me years to overcome. Mix severe depression with a raging libido in a self-loathing, virgin teenager and you end up with a very lethal combination.

It all kicked off a week after prom. Still feeling insecure about my lack of hair, I tried to improve my appearance with eyeliner and earrings. Feeling somewhat good, I headed over to Leslie's for our regular Friday night fiasco of drinking and roaming around town. That night I got to know Jeff, Leslie's good-looking roommate, who I often shied away from most visits to the apartment. For some reason, he was paying more attention to me than usual. He was giving me compliments and laughing at jokes I made. As I observed his unexpected attention, I thought to myself, *"He can't actually be into me? Can he?"*

I'm not sure how it happened, but I ended up in his room, sitting on his bed, talking about some random thing. He stopped me halfway through a sentence by stroking my face.

"You are so beautiful, Cara. I hope you know that!"

It seemed sincere; I just didn't believe him. Although I can't deny it, in the moment it felt good to feel beautiful. We started kissing and, before I knew it, I was having sex. It seemed so natural, yet such an absurd act, allowing someone to enter my body. It hurt, but I wouldn't admit it and couldn't help feel some regret that this moment didn't take place with someone I loved. Was this as good as it was going to get for me? How did I get from being close to death and angels to this? My head swirled with thoughts, flashbacks, moments that were so unrelated and removed from this moment; I couldn't quite understand where they were coming from. Then, as he was about to climax, the thoughts became clear and I could only think of one thing. "God, please forgive me!"

# CHAPTER TWENTY-EIGHT

# THE SMILE

October 14, 2004

Dear Cole,

Remember, in the last entry, when I told you that when you trust the Universe everything will work out. Well, good things have happened for us since then. Mommy had a meeting with the big boss of the company and I knew it was a competition between me and my co-worker. Now your mother is not one for competing but, at that moment, I fought for this job and I won! All I know is that, if we don't have this money coming in, the line of credit I owe from Australia will not get paid off and that money is our ticket to getting off social assistance. So now I am working 40 hours a week! Horraaay!

Your Nana and Papa went away for a week to visit your Uncle Chris in Montreal, and it was very good for me to have time to myself to think and just be. Sometimes it's really hard to be mothered when you are trying to make decisions as a mother. I am currently looking into taking a tourism course when you're about 10 months old. I think this will give me more job opportunities to support the both of us. Plus, I really like to help people. I want to take you traveling with me, but your grandparents say that taking you away from your family will be terrible. I'm noticing a lot of guilt comes with this new role as a mother. I so desperately don't want to screw you up! I want the best for you, always know that.

I think of how hard it must have been on my parents, dealing with me as a teenager, especially that summer. Unfortunately things went from bad to worse, but I always want you to remember something, my sweet little boy, forgiveness is the key to freedom. Forgiving yourself is something people often overlook, but it is a fundamental component to unlocking a blissful heart.


## <u>The Wrong Move</u>

Obviously I never told my mother what was happening in my world or what went on in that apartment. It was no different than any other college apartment with friends stopping over on a regular basis, blades cooking on the stove and an endless amount of liquor being consumed. In a desperate attempt to help me get over the depression, Mom agreed to let me move in with Leslie and a few friends for the summer.

Jeff had moved out shortly after our experience and, although nothing ever came of it, he always treated me with respect. I was always so grateful for that.

I was so excited about my first experience living on my own. I never actually thought I would live long enough to see this day and felt a surge of independence course through my veins. I was so happy Mom let me go and I knew how scary it must have been for her to make that decision.

We crammed our three single beds into one room, the second room being taken by Laura and her double bed. Laughing and carrying on, the four of us excitedly prepared our new space for the summer together. It was my first taste of freedom and separation from my parents, even if it was only down the street. I did not take it for granted and remembered how only months before I couldn't even have a shower without a nurse or my mother knocking on the door every time they heard the soap drop. Now I was on my own.

The responsibilities of an independent life seemed impossible. I totally depended on my parents for all the money to be there, and I continually grocery shopped in their pantry. All in all, I think we all knew that I had been given a second chance and all my parents wanted for me was to be happy. I didn't want to let them down but, the reality was, I was far from happy. Something was happening to me that I couldn't describe to anyone.

If I were to summarize that summer for you, I can only say that it was the worst summer of my life. I have an extremely detailed memory. I can remember where people were standing, what they were wearing and how the situation played out. That summer was the first time I ever lost my memory.

My friends began to tell me things I was doing and saying that I had no recollection of and, truthfully, were so unlike me that I felt they were talking about someone else.

Somehow, I kept falling deeper and deeper into situations that were more than unhealthy—they were dangerous. Unfortunately, I found out how dangerous in the worst possible way.

I had a crush on this guy, Alex, with whom I'd graduated. One night we hooked up at a party and I was surprised at how easily I just let it happen. Then, at another party, I let Sam. A week later, it was his brother, then his brother's friend the next night. I wasn't really sure why this was happening or how the ability to say "no" became lost in my voice. The truth is, I became really great at doing something I hated and I couldn't understand why I kept letting it happen over and over again.

Each time it played out the same way. The guy would pay attention to me and I would feel pretty, as if I had something the other girls didn't. For a moment, I would feel powerful, in control and desirable. The next thing I knew, we would end up in his room, clothes thrown to the floor and, just as casually as if we were shaking hands, he would end up inside me. With his entry into my body, all power would be gone and, to cover up for hating the moment, I would make all the proper noises to make him think he was a sex god. Waiting for him to climax, I would stare at the ceiling, each time having the same repetitive thought, "Please, God, forgive me!"

I drank more to drown the sadness and prayed that my crush, Alex, would just sweep me off my feet, tell me he loved me just the way I was, and make love to me the way I always dreamed. Instead, I turned into a slut.

I don't remember the darkness that came out of my mouth, but my friends told me that I was very vocal about how much I hated myself. Sometimes I couldn't believe what they told I said because I had no memory of it. It was at that time I decided to get myself back on track.

I began ignoring my current crush and stopped sleeping with people. If they really wanted to be with me, they would have to work harder for it. As Mom always said, "Why buy the cow when you can get the milk for free?" I felt good about this new perspective and really started to feel better.

One night, at my friend, Sam's, party, down the street, I ran into a bunch of people from school I hadn't seen all summer. The place was packed, wall to wall, smoke-filled, drinks were plentiful and everyone was having a blast. I saw Alex in the corner of the room. We began playing the game: I notice you noticing me, but I'm not going to let on that I notice you noticing me. Finally he came over and asked if he could speak with me in the washroom. I should have known he wanted more, but I gave him the benefit of the doubt because I liked him so much.

As we entered the stall, he inched towards me, saying, "Why are you ignoring me? Don't you want to be with me anymore?"

I was trying to stay true to myself and turn the corner on this horrible pattern I had created. I tried to play it cool, even though it didn't really fit my demeanour.

"If you want to be with me, why not stop ignoring me and ask me out?" I retorted.

He came up from behind me and whispered in my ear, "I know you want to be with me. Why are you pretending you don't?"

Chills ran up my spine—I was both turned on and extremely pissed off. I decided to end this conversation and I turned to leave when everything began happening in fast motion. He grabbed my hands and pinned them up over my head so I couldn't get free.

"Alex, this isn't funny. Let me go!" I demanded, trying to free myself from his grip but, before I knew it, I could feel him ripping my pants down from behind. Why couldn't I get my wrists free? This wasn't really happening!

"No!" I repeated, but it was too late; he had already shoved himself inside me and this time it hurt. As he made grunting noises, still holding my wrists, I felt he knew I had given up. I was scared and I thought, if I just gave in, it would be over sooner. It had been less than five minutes, but it felt like an eternity.

Someone banged on the door, saying, "Cara, you okay? Open the door! Are you okay? Let me in!"

The intrusion freaked Alex out and he pulled out of me, zipped up his pants and I quickly pulled up mine, in a reactive state of consciousness when the door burst open.

We left the room and I headed for the sofa. I kept smiling, pretending that nothing happened.

"What did just happen? Did that just happen?" My mind raced.

Shannon, the girl who had opened the door, sat next to me.

She grabbed my hand and softly asked, "Honey, what happened in there? Are you okay?"

As if someone had taken over my body, I began smiling.

"Oh, yeah," I grinned from ear to ear. "Don't worry about it; it was nothing!"

I stood up to put my jacket on, trying my best to ignore Alex staring at me from the other side of the room. I gave Shannon a hug and left.

All I could hear were my footsteps shuffling beneath me, one foot in front of the other, faster and faster, until I was in a full sprint. I could finally see my apartment door.

I smiled again as I entered our place to greet my roommates. I appeared rational, calm, in control, but my insides were trembling. I excused myself to our bedroom where I robotically prepared for bed. Pajamas, check; medication, check; brush teeth, check. I crawled under the covers seeking solace but, instead, felt shame and the pounding question I didn't want to contemplate assaulted the my brain like a hammer, *"Was I just raped?"*

I wanted to sleep, but the covers felt like wet shackles on my filthy body.

*"Did I ask for it?"* I questioned, over and over. *"I must have, I wasn't drinking but he knew I liked him. I had sex with him before so he must have gotten the wrong idea."*

My mind raced. I wanted to forget it ever happened, but the moment played on repeat. I could still feel his sharp penis stabbing me, his hands pinning mine over my head.

*"I'm such a slut!"* I told myself as my prayer for sleep was finally answered.

So began another girl's journey of surviving sexual violence. Completely unaware of the damage it had done, I soon became aware a few weeks later.

# CHAPTER TWENTY-NINE

# SHANE: GRACED BY GOD

October 17, 2004

Dear Cole,

As I reflect on this time in my life I find it ironic that the other day I ran into the mother of my friend, Shane, at a party. Ironic because he is the earth angel I was just about to write about in this story. Remember Shane, the boyfriend whom the girls got so excited about when I was seventeen?

His mother and I caught up and I asked her about Shane; it had been so long since I'd seen him. She told he me was doing well, but giggled a little about his hair and wished he would someday cut it off.

When Shane was in his twenties, something spoke to him about living the spiritual life he desired. He told me how the Rastafarian religion found him and from that point on he was determined to live a life that followed this path. Many people thought that he became this way because he lived in Jamaica for six months but, the truth is, he had become devoted to Rastafarianism almost a year before.

Shane drank and smoked cigarettes like so many other young people. He shared with me how this was a Babylonian life and a cleansing was needed. Never had I experienced anyone go through as much peer pressure as Shane did. His friends just couldn't believe he'd changed and continued to offer him drink after drink, cigarette after cigarette, but Shane turned them down consistently. I was in complete awe of his determination and inspired by his will to change.

I knew that people didn't understand what he was doing or that being a Rasta was more than just the stereotype of a Reggae-infused, weed-smoking, dreadlock-wearing costume. Shane taught me about his organic way of eating, how he never ate anything off the vine or any scavengers of the sea, and how cutting his hair was considered desecrating his body.

Years later, when we lived together during my last year of university I watched him read his Bible every night; he truly exuded dedication.

Now, with his dreadlocks down his back, never to be cut, I understood his mother's wishes for a clean-cut son with traditional beliefs but, the thing is, sometimes the most beautiful things come in the most unusual packages. Shane is a good man, a really good man. I wanted her to know she did an amazing job. I felt it was time to share with his mother what Shane did for me because, if it were you, I would want to know that you were the reflection of the things I taught you. Shane Delorey saved my life!

## A Dark Night of the Soul

After the rape, I sunk into a depression that almost ended my life. My friends didn't understand what was happening to me and I didn't understand either. So young and naive—how could I possibly comprehend the depth of the darkness in which I had placed myself?

One night, Alex showed up at our apartment and, for whatever reason I agreed for him to come inside and speak with me. As we went into my friend's room, she warned me not to "do anything" in her bed or she would be super pissed.

I closed the door behind us. How was it possible I still had feelings for this horrible person after what he had done to me? He began apologizing and trying to get near me, but I couldn't take it and I asked him to leave. Unfortunately, it was not before my friend knocked on the door, suspecting that we were heavy into it.

I trembled, my mind raced, and my thoughts were dark. After he left, I sat on the sofa of our crowded living room and cried, but nobody paid any attention. They were on the phone with Jessica, a friend who was threatening to kill herself. I knew Jessica was full of shit, that it was a dramatic attempt to get attention, but my friends continued to ignore me and focus on her.

Laura grabbed my hand and stroked it as I wept silently in the corner. Why did they not care? Why were the ignoring me? A cloud of hopelessness choked me until I couldn't breathe. I wanted out! Here they were, focusing on Jessica, and I actually wanted to kill myself. With that thought I stood up, the decision having been made. This was not worth it anymore. The pain of my own thoughts, the lack of control, the confusion, the pain, the pain, the pain! All I could feel was pain! I wanted it gone, I needed it gone! I was willing to do anything to make that happen and, with no plan on how, I focused on just getting it done.

"Maybe I could drown myself," I thought, desperate to find something quickly before I lost my nerve and had to live this way forever.

I walked out the door and knew I was never coming back.

Closing the door behind me, I didn't see Shane sitting on the deck in the darkness. I think he sensed the urgency that radiated from me and I briskly walked away from the apartment. He ran after me.

"Cara, wait! Where are you going?" he called, trying to catch up with me.

"Never mind," I hollered back at him. "Leave me alone, Shane. It's none of your business!"

Why now? I was ready to end this pain forever and Shane was just getting in the way. He didn't understand what it was like to be stuck in this body, in this experience. God gave me a second chance at life and what did I do to thank Him, I screwed it up! I didn't deserve God's love, His grace, His forgiveness. I made a promise to Him and I totally let him down. How could He ever forgive me?

"Cara, please slow down, please," Shane pleaded with me.

"No, Shane," I argued. "You can't stop me; this is out of your control."

Shane understood the seriousness of this moment and what I was planning. He inched closer to me.

"Hear me out," he pleaded. "Just come and sit with me on the deck for a bit and talk and, if you don't like what I have to say, you can go. Okay?"

I didn't want to talk with him, but his eyes were so sincere. I might have had one thing on my mind, but his kindness briefly melted my emotional wall.

"Fine," I agreed with reluctance.

As we made our way to the deck, Shane began asking me what was happening and why I was so sad?

With those two simple questions, my whole self caved in. Exhausted and defeated, I felt I had nothing left to give. I began crying uncontrollably.

"I don't want to live anymore, Shane. I can't take it! The pain is too much!"

He wrapped his arms around me and I cried on his shoulder.

"Cara, you can't leave me, you are much too important to our lives to think of such a thing. It will get better, I promise," he reassured me as he rubbed my back, trying his best to ease my pain.

"You don't understand, Shane," I argued. "I have let everyone down. I let God down and I let my parents down. I feel so lonely!"

The tears flowed freely, my body trembling as if I were in a full tonic clonic seizure.

"I know, Cara. I know you are sad and that we might not understand what it's like for you right now, but I want you to reconsider because there is one thing I know for sure, I need you in my life! Stay for me, please! Stay for me!"

He continued to hold me while I released all the pain and heartache that my young body held in for months—the surgery, not graduating, the depression, the rape. It all spilled out onto Shane's shirt and he embraced me with a love that I will never forget. He truly was one of my best friends and, that night, by loving me, he saved my life.

## CHAPTER THIRTY

# THE EYE OF THE BEHOLDER

Oct 19, 2004

Dear Cole,

It's only a few more months until I get to meet you face to face. I am so excited and so are your grandparents. I've been working really hard to find opportunities for us so that we can live comfortably. I'm going to have to work harder than I've ever worked in my life, but I don't mind because it's for the both of us. My mother and father want to help me start a photography business in town. I don't know how I'm going to pull this off and still have a place to live, but I'd like to take a shot at it. It's scary because I'm not exactly the ideal business person. I'm what you call the "artsy flighty type." It's a leap of faith, but I think I can do it if I set my mind to it. I never wanted to live here, that's one thing I know for sure. Your mother has had some bad memories in this town and sometimes that little girl emerges wearing a mask of fear.

Lately I've been feeling okay about this place. We have so many friends and family living here who love and support us. People are beginning to know me more in a professional way and I have the possibility to network. I will just have to wait and see, I guess. Patience is not a virtue I possess with ease.

It occurs to me that I have been at a crossroads like this before: the summer after my surgery when my mother tried to convince me to go back to school and I would immediately start to cry. I was afraid of failure then and I overcame that, so maybe I should not be so afraid of failure anymore. Maybe failure is in the eye of the beholder. I mean, what is failure anyway? I remeber a story I once heard about Thomas Edison, who invented the light bulb. It took him over two thousand tries to get his invention right and, when a young journalist was interviewing him, he inquired, "Mr. Edison, how does it feel to have failed over two thousand times?"

Thomas Edison looked at him, shocked, and simply replied, "Young man, I invented the light bulb; it just happened to be a two-thousand-step process."

What a great way to think about opportunity when other people view it as failure. I didn't fail then, so maybe I should just continue to take the leap of faith. It works for me better than fear anyway. I must have faith.

## The Stranger who Changed My Life

The summer was finally coming to an end and I decided, after my close call with suicide, it was time to move home. I tried not to think about the rape and distanced myself from Alex, which was challenging to do in a small town.

My mother and I spoke about everything, but I never told her about what happened. I couldn't bear hearing anything like, "You shouldn't have been there," or "Was there alcohol involved?"

These were things I often hear from my mother's generation that must have been taught by their parents, and I can't help but get super angry and defiant when I hear it. I mean, really? Seriously? How is it that, when a girl gets raped, they react like she brought it on herself? I was at a party with my friends, I wasn't even drunk, I just wanted to hear what he had to say, then BAM. I become the all-you-can-eat buffet for sexual gluttony. *"Yep, I totally deserved it,"* I sarcastically thought. I don't think I will ever understand that rationale.

As soon as I returned home, my mother was on my case about going back to school and graduating.

"Are you out of your mind?" I said. "Mom, I can't do it again, I can't!"

"Cara, it's just one more year; you will be so happy that you did it," she pleaded.

I was so tired. Not graduating with my class had completely deflated my drive to go to art school. I had given up. I just wasn't sure I had it in me anymore, studying so much and then losing all the information from a seizure just before the exam. The feeling of staring at the paper, not understanding any of the questions, but knowing that at some point I did. I just felt so stupid and I wasn't sure if I could live with that feeling anymore.

Every couple of days my mother would try again, but I would cry at the mention of school. I realized I had created a full-blown phobia of failure and, just like someone afraid of the dark, I only wanted to stand in the light. Then one day, out of the blue, I met a woman who changed my life forever.

I don't know if my mother planned this or not, but, if she did, I will be grateful until the day I die. It is always the simplest gestures that change the course of a person's life, whether it is a sentence, conversation, a random act of kindness from a stranger or someone who simply listens. Whatever the trigger, it has become very clear to me that one thought can change the world.

My mother owned a tole-painting shop that she ran out of her spare room. We often had a lot of traffic in the house due to workshops or customers buying gifts.

One day, my mother called me in to introduce me to a woman named Trina. Mom shared with her how I had just come through a challenging time in my life, that I felt defeated and tired, and that I wasn't interested in going back to school.

I rolled my eyes at my mother and couldn't believe she was sharing this so candidly with a stranger. My eyes were downcast, ashamed that I had given up so easily and I didn't want to see the judgment in Trina's eyes.

When my eyes met hers, all I saw was pure compassion. She took my hand and asked if she could speak with me alone outside. Shocked by this gesture, I agreed.

Once outside, Trina told me her story of struggle, how she too had overcome great difficulty and how many people also told her that she "couldn't do it." She never listened. Trina leaped over those obstacles with perseverance and she told me that when the naysayers wanted to speak to her she smiled gently and put on her headphones to drown them out. In the end, the naysayers went away and only supporters remained. She went on to become the head director of the company she now works for and has succeeded far beyond her wildest dreams.

She squeezed my hand and said something I will never forget:

"Cara, you have been through so much in your life. You have worked so hard to stay alive, to fight for your life. You are young and have your whole life ahead of you. Don't you want to give yourself the opportunity that you deserve, that you fought so hard for?"

Her words went straight to my heart and tears trickled down my cheeks. I felt she truly understood, from her own experience, what I was feeling, facing and fearing. All I could do was nod. The next day, one month away from my nineteenth birthday, I signed up for my last year of high school. Even though I was afraid and embarrassed to be going back, I decided it was time to get busy living. So that was what I began to do—started to live.

# CHAPTER THIRTY-ONE

# IN THE LIGHT OF CHANGE

November 4, 2004

Dear Cole,

It dawned on me, this morning, how quickly life can change from one year to the next. On Halloween night, I realized that twelve months prior I was standing in front of a class of Korean students dressed as a clown. I remember that day well and how funny it was that everyone was frightened of me because they don't celebrate Halloween in their country. It is amazing when you look at those twelve months and realize that I was teaching in Korea, lived and studied wood sculpture in the rain forest of Australia, and now am pregnant with you—all in that short period of time. What a blessing that year has been.

I have recurring dreams that I am traveling in Australia looking for Jason but, when I finally find him, I can't get him to talk to me; he just ignores me. I didn't realize until now how much the real scenario screwed with my head. God, I hope that someday he comes around and realizes how much he is missing out on, not having you in his life. He will not see you grow and develop into the person I know you will be. Please, God, help him wake up!

You see, sweetheart, these times are strange. Each generation is different than the one before. Things like commitment and relationships seem few and far between. I miss the idea of dating, the guy wanting to get to know the girl by taking her to dinner or a movie. Where did that go? I really miss the idea of romance. For instance, when you do something small for the person you care for just because you were thinking of them. Our generation has gotten so caught up in fear from all the divorces of the 1980s that taking a chance seems too risky. I will never give up on the dream that someone wonderful is out there for me. Until I find him, I`ll be happy with just the two of us.

Mom just called me here at work to tell me that we have a crib! I was so excited because I really wanted to prepare my room for you. I found out the other day that I will be having my second ultrasound on November 27 to see if the placenta has moved. If it doesn't, I might have to be on bed rest for the remainder of my pregnancy. Sure, I will do anything for you, but my reaction was WHAT—lying around for two months when I'm usually so active! I keep giving you Reiki to see if I can move it myself. God, I hope it works.

Every day I get closer to the delivery date, I get more excited and nervous. I hope I will have lots of patience. I`m going to try my best. Really, I have no choice in the end, so I best chill for now.

I`m going to Sydney on Wednesday to see your great-grandfather, Joe, who`s sick with cancer. I hope he will hold on so he can get the chance to hold you in his arms. No matter if he`s here on earth or not, he will still look at you with pride and joy.

Joe is a kindred spirit. Since I met him in 1997, he always seems so proud to have me in his life. You see, baby, your mommy was adopted and the story is quite interesting.

When your grandmother, Maureen, was nineteen, she became pregnant while getting her textiles degree at St. Francis Xavier University. Your grandfather, David, whom she was so in love with, was an officer in the military and the situation was not ideal. They were too young.

Maureen never really wanted to give me up but, back in 1977, unless you were married, a pregnancy out of wedlock was a no-no. Her family owned the funeral parlour in North Sydney and had a bit of an elite role in the community, from what I gather, so Maureen was sent off to Halifax for the majority of her pregnancy then had me in Sydney and was back to school a few weeks later.

It was really hard for her and David, but life has a way of working out. She and David fell deeper in love after the pregnancy and got married a few years later. I have three siblings: Angela, Anthony and Steven. Things began to unfold when I was nineteen. I went searching for them and some answers to the many questions I had about myself.

After finding out their contact information, through child welfare services, I decided to call them. I remember that first phone call being the most difficult call I have ever made. I mean, what do you say, "Hi, it's your long-lost daughter. How are things?" I honestly don't know what we talked about, probably the awkwardness of it all, but I felt a sense of relief and fulfillment that has never left me.

I went to visit them about six months later after getting to know everyone via email. I know it sounds weird, but just through email I could see so much of myself in my birth dad, David, even in the way he wrote.

I took that long, snowy bus drive to New Brunswick and thought about my Mom and Dad who raised me and how scary it must have been to let me go on that bus alone, going to meet strangers, hoping they were as nice as they seemed in their emails.

The snow was so bad that day that, when they came to pick me up, they drove half an hour in the wrong direction and I had to wait in suspense in a gas station and keep my mind busy reading magazines. Every time the door opened, I peeked out the corner of my eye, wondering if it was them and pretending not to notice the door opening. Finally, I got a tap on my shoulder and looked up into eyes that resembled a mirror, something I had never experienced before. They hugged me so tightly and then we got in their car and I went back to their home to meet my siblings.

Your aunt, Angela, was only eight years old at the time and your uncles, Anthony and Stephen, were 12 and 14, respectively. I can't imagine how strange it was for them to find out they had a sister. I always knew I was adopted, but they had just found out about me.

After having dinner and looking at pictures, we went off to bed. That night was so significant to all of us because it was the first time we were all under one roof as a family. It was beautiful.

When you are adopted and find your family, you don't just find one or two members, you end up inheriting cousins, grandparents, aunts and uncles.

I met Joe and Virgina, my grandparents, and I could tell the situation had really hurt them, in different ways, as well. Joe was so proud of me and one night he whispered in my ear, "I never wanted to let you go." Don't get me wrong, sweetheart, I don't think your great-grandmother wanted to give me up either, but I think with the times they were living in, it was just expected.

Virigina always loved me, but she too was adopted and her mother was cruel to her as she grew up, often threatening her that if she didn't do what she was told she would be "sent back" to where she came from. I can't imagine how traumatizing that was for my grandmother. She did the best she could with what she knew at the time and everything happens for a reason.

I feel so lucky to be living in a time when things are changing quite a bit. I have so much more support than Maureen had in making her choice.

It still is not easy, but at least people don't put such a badge of shame on you like the big "A" in the scarlet letter, like they did when my mother was pregnant with me.

Someday, I hope to tell you a little bit more about this story but, for now, I have to tell you it is one of the major reasons I chose life for you. I got to witness firsthand how life can heal. I know that we are going to be okay together. I can feel it and I know it in my mind's eye. It's sometimes difficult trying to convince everyone else that this is the case.

# CHAPTER TWENTY-TWO

# IN HER SHOES

November 9, 2004

Dear Cole,

I got into a huge fight with my grandmother and it was heartbreaking for me. It is strange how, in the most awkward situations, there can be such moments of release and healing.

We were out at the cottage having dinner on the patio when somehow the topic of relationships came up. My sister, who is only 15, told me that she knew she was probably going to get divorced. I looked at her and felt sad that she had already given up on love and she was so young; it really displayed how times have changed. My grandmother pipes in and starts directing the conversation at me, saying that "none of you knows how to commit; you all give up so easily on relationships."

I was very offended by this remark because the truth was I did want to commit, it's just that the situation is two sided and I wasn't about to stay with a guy who was treating me badly. Her remarks seemed to be directed at me and I became super sensitive to what she was saying and how she was treating me that evening. I can't describe it, but it was almost as if she couldn't look at me, as if she was faced with history repeating itself, only this time I was keeping the baby.

Looking at her, I stood up from the table, replying, "What would you know about it Virginia? You married Joe. The day you can introduce me to someone even half as wonderful as he, then we can talk."

I left and got into the car with my brother.

I was so angry and hurt by her body language and words (I only touched the surface). I walked into the house and I called your Nana in Antigonish. I realized quickly what was happening to me. It was as if I was floating above the situation and felt my birth mother's pain of giving me up, what she had to go through in being strong while faced with judgment and not wanting to give me up. My heart broke for her.

The next morning, I sat in the kitchen where Maureen was having her morning tea. I started crying and told her how I felt and how sorry I was that she had to experience the trauma of her choice and how brave she was to give me up.

She grasped her cup and started to weep. Then she jumped up and flung her arms around me. "I am so grateful to have you in my life," she cried. From that moment, we moved forward together.


## Dreams, Drive and Determination

It had been a while since I had a premonition or experience with my angels. I often wondered if it was because I had gone down such a bad path, or maybe the brain surgery had removed my ability to communicate on this level. Then one night I met my spirit guide.

Truthfully, I didn't know what a spirit guide was at this time, but I now understand that it is a spiritual partner who accompanies you throughout your life, giving you guidance. When I met my spirit guide, Seth, I didn't know the significance he was to have in my life. I just knew that somehow it was very important.

Three weeks before school was to begin, I began to have doubt. Just before going to bed, I asked for guidance and that's the night I met Seth.

I awoke in a field, but I couldn't understand how I got there because the last thing I remembered was going to sleep in my bed. I sat up and felt the grass beneath my hands and the prickle of the blades under my fingers. I became completely mesmerized by the colour. It was as if the grass sparkled and was a brighter shade of any green I had ever seen.

The field, in which I sat, was luscious and the breeze, I swear, sounded like it was singing.

"Singing grass?" I thought. "Now this is a trippy dream."

Standing up, I walked towards a glowing stream of water about five feet away from me. On the other side of the stream was a hill that glistened with the same grass, only it was interspersed with flowers I had never seen before and colours I honestly didn't recognize. The more I stared at them the more they seemed to speak to me. Flowers with personalities! All I could think was, "Amazing!"

I looked down at the stream—was that even water? It flowed all along the edge of the hill and it too sparkled and sang and I became fixated on how clear it was. It invoked a feeling of love while I stared at it. I proceeded to put my foot in the water but something stopped me. I'm not sure what it was, but it was almost a knowing that I was not supposed to cross the river. Just as that thought sunk in, I looked up and saw a man walking down the hill towards me. He wore a pair of jeans, a plaid shirt, had short, wavy, brown hair and was barefoot. The man appeared to be in his thirties and, as he drew closer, I noticed his eyes were a vivid ice blue.

When he reached the stream, he waded through it to the other side, greeting me with a loving and embracing smile. The moment he smiled, my whole being recognized him and I wrapped my arms around him in complete and utter joy. The reunion was reciprocated and he picked me up and swung me around, so pleased that I remembered him. Strangely, I did remember him, but I wasn't sure how, as if there were an invisible veil separating me from my memories. Reading my thoughts, he chuckled and said, "I love how accepting you always are in each of your experiences, Cara."

His words were so genuine and he displayed such love for me.

"My name is Seth," he answered my thoughts. "We have known each other a very long time and I help you learn on your journey."

Seth's words invoked memories that I could see and could feel and I continued to feel overjoyed by his presence and our reunion.

He held my hand and we walked along the stream, enjoying each other's company. Finally I spoke up. "What am I supposed to do, Seth?" I asked, like a child seeking guidance from a parent.

He stopped and turned to face me, looking me in the eye and into my soul. His eyes were the most beautiful I have ever seen. Then I remembered that, I had been here before, when I was six and had the seizure.

Pleased that I remembered, Seth smiled and nodded in confirmation.

"Is this heaven? Am I dead?" I asked, a little surprised by what I was remembering, but calm at the same time.

"No," Seth assured, "we are at a meeting place that connects our worlds; that was why you knew not to cross the water, Cara. You are very much alive."

I let out a sigh of relief, which I found interesting because only months before I had been completely ready to leave my body and head home.

"You are doing exactly what you planned," Seth said. "We are all very proud of you. Your job is so important, Cara, and you are meant to do so much more than you ever imagined. Your life is meaningful and I am with you every step of the way."

Again I became flooded with memories and I understood what he meant. He continued to affirm. "You may not always remember what to do, but you will remember that I am here to help you."

It was nice not to be alone, and I felt silly for feeling like I had been alone before. He was always there. Seth gave me one more smile and said, "Go now Cara. I am with you."

Seth squeezed my hand and I awoke with a jolt. I lay there, my heart racing, my mind calm and blissful. It was as if I had just had the rush of my life and Seth was still in the room with me, which he probably was. I knew that my life had purpose. The fear of school was replaced with determination and drive that fueled a fire in my heart. I had a purpose and I knew that I would never let the thought of giving up take the lead ever again! I would succeed and Seth was there to help me.

# CHAPTER THIRTY-THREE

# ART, I LOVE YOU

November 12, 2004

Dear Cole,

I had my photography exhibition at St. F.X University and it went well. Any kind of exposure is good at this point and I look forward to more exhibitions in the future.

Man, this third trimester is filled with surprises. I keep having back spasms during the night and the girls at work keep laughing at me. It's because I always try to laugh off my pain so people end up laughing with me. They keep joking that it never seems like I am really pregnant because my personality screams single and free. My question to them is, "Well, aren't I?"

I took the Canon Rebel digital camera out on Tuesday and was very impressed. It's a lot of money to invest, but I guess if I want my career to go anywhere I have to take that leap. You are going to laugh at this entry someday because that camera is going to seem like a dinosaur. I can't even keep up with the technology; it's crazy to think about what it's going to be like in 26 years! Yikes!

## The Art of Focus

The morning of the first day of school, I decided that, if I were going to face high school again at age nineteen, I was going to use it as an opportunity to achieve my dream. I was going to get into NSCAD.

I grabbed my new sketchbook and made a commitment that it would become my permanent companion. I would draw everything; I would live art, breath art and sleep art, if that is what I had to do to get into that school. No more bullshit, no more drama; it was time to focus on what I wanted and make it happen.

I was happy to find out that a few of my school friends also stayed behind to upgrade. All I could think was, "Thank God I'm not alone!"

The first few months were physically and emotionally trying. I was still dealing with depression and getting my medication balanced but, overall, I was feeling good about my future. I kept my promise to myself and drew everything, and took every art class I could, even if it meant I was the youngest person among a geriatric crew. I learned so much from my older mentors and they respected my drive and passion.

School had become a more positive place than I first thought. Now that I was no longer having seizures, my memory was intact and, in my first set of exams I made 80 percent on my biology exam. I couldn't believe it when my teacher, Mr. Barker, handed it back to me and I could see the look of pride in his expression as he shared my accomplishment. Tears formed at the edges of my eyes. It was a personal confirmation that I was actually intelligent. I, Cara Jones, learning disabled, never having graduated from high school, made an 80 percent! Could it be that everything they had said to me—those Doctors and teachers who expressed doubt for my future and labeled it "unrealistic"—were full of shit?

Holding the biology paper in my hand, I knew that life was just waiting for me to take part and make something of myself.

I realized that year how important the role of a teacher is in a young person's life. I had watched teachers fight for me, believe in me and argue with those who gave up faith in me so easily. Those teachers go on to change the world through their empowerment of students such as myself. I could write forever about every teacher I have ever had who influenced my life in a positive way but, that final year, two stood out in my mind the most.

Mr. Barker, my biology teacher, saw my determination to get into NSCAD and helped me achieve my goal. Pulling me aside one day, he made a proposal for my final biology project.

"Cara, I know you have been through a lifetime of struggle in just one year and I see how hard you are working. I want to help you."

Sitting down in the blue plastic chair next to me, he folded his hands on the desk and turned to me.

"How would you like to paint the cupboard doors in our class with any topic in biology and present that topic as your final project?"

I was dumbfounded by his suggestion, as well as extremely grateful. I couldn't believe he was thinking out of the box and allowing my creative mind to express itself through a science project. What an amazing teacher!

As the months went on, my mother also became invested in my dream of attending art school and offered to pay for local artist, Vicky MacLean, to help me with my portfolio.

Each week, I went to her studio and she helped me understand what the jury was looking for when accepting students, how I needed to create work that was "messy" and inspired, not perfect and not always complete. It was nice to learn from her and develop my portfolio and, as the weeks passed, my work began to resemble that of a professional artist. I could see my dream coming to fruition. All I had to do now was write my entrance essay. As I sat in front of the computer, I wondered how I would explain so much of how I felt, experienced and desired for my future in only five hundred words. Here is what I came up with:

### Nova Scotia College of Art and Design
### Admissions Statement: Cara Jones

**Art is something I've always enjoyed but, over the past three or four years, it has become a part of me. Whenever I feel a certain emotion, whether it be happy or sad, and I can't quite express it to anyone, I release my feelings in an artistic creation. It could be anything from creative writing to conjuring an image in a visual aspect. You see, life for me has been a roller-coaster ride, but the one thing that has always remained constant has been my ability to express myself.**

**During my senior year in high school, students were encouraged to consider what our goals might be for the future. I knew, whatever it was I chose, it would encompass the art industry. After consulting my guidance counsellor and reading about the Nova Scotia College of Art and Design, I knew this was the institute where I wanted to further my education.**

Having this goal felt good, but I realized that, even though I did have talent, my work was very amateur, so I signed up for as many art workshops as I could. These workshops covered such areas as photography, watercolours and sketching. I began enhancing my knowledge and experience.

With my future planned out, I thought that it would be easy from that point on. Easy was anything but what it was!

You see, in order for you to truly understand what I've been through in keeping this goal to be educated at NSCAD, I must share a personal part of my life. I have a medical condition called epilepsy which I have struggled with since the age of six. During grades eleven and twelve, my condition became progressively worse.

Trying so very hard to achieve well academically was pretty much impossible for me because my memory would be erased every day due to the seizures. I battled emotional distress because of the constant fight to be as normal as my friends were but, in the back of my mind, my future looked bleak. Then the most miraculous thing happened. I was chosen to be a candidate for neurosurgery to correct my condition. I went to London, Ontario, where I underwent extensive observation and two successful brain surgeries. After a forty-eight-day stay, I was able to return home.

Upon returning home, graduation became an unrealistic goal. Because of the amount of time I missed from school, I had to drop a course in order to catch up with my other studies. I was thus unable to graduate with my class. This had a profound effect on my way of thinking and I wanted to give up on school forever. After trying so hard, and not doing well over the years, I had developed a phobia of school. After much encouragement and advice from friends and family, I made one of the biggest decisions of my life: to give grade twelve another try. It was one of the best decision I've ever made.

Because I no longer had seizures, I was able to think more clearly and retain what I was studying. This gave me a new sense of self-esteem and, for the first time ever, I realized that my efforts were finally beginning to pay off.

My goal to attend NSCAD was now within reach and my future no longer seemed bleak.

As you can tell from the information I have shared, determination has played a huge part in my life. I never gave up on my dream, even though the temptation was there, and that, in itself, shows what I can offer your school.

I feel I possess talent, but to describe to you in a few pages how much art means to me is difficult. It has helped me through many hard times and I thirst for the knowledge to learn and understand it to a greater extent.

I look forward with anticipation to an interview for admission to your school.

Sincerely,
Cara Jones
1997

CHAPTER THIRTY-FOUR

# OPTIMISTIC FRANKENSTEIN

January 1, 2005

Dear Cole,

Happy New Year, Cole! This is going to be an eventful year for both of us. You are coming into the world and I am going to grow more as a person this year, taking on this role of mother. The time grows near to our first meeting.

It's been awhile since I have written in this journal; I find I am overwhelmed preparing for your arrival.

The other night while in the shower, I caressed my belly and announced to you, "Okay, Cole, whenever you are ready you can come out."

I swear you heard me because about an hour later I started to get really bad Braxton Hicks contractions that lasted a long time. I have been having them constantly over the past three days, but it's a good sign, it means you are on your way.

The other day, I went to social services to see what kind of help they can give us. With unemployment benefits, I will be living off a total of $738.00 a month, not very much at all.

Mom got really scared for me, but I told her that even though it's going to be hard, we'll be okay because it's only temporary. I let her know the one great thing that you have on your side is that you have me as a mother and I am an extremely hard worker. I will work hard to give you all the things you need even though it won't be easy. I promise we will get through this.

My optimism drives my mother crazy but, at the same time, I get a kick out of it. She was the one who instilled the "never say die" attitude I possess. It's that attitude that has kept me alive all these years. I have become her worst optimistic nightmare! I just don't see the point in sitting around having a pity party. As you can see from my story, I spent the majority of my teenage years as the host of my very own pity party and that frame of mind gets you nowhere. Faith gets you everywhere. Faith keeps you going.

I kept thinking you were going to be born early, but now I don't think so. Your personality so far has been very confusing. Sometimes I'm convinced you are a boy and then it feels like you're a girl. I even feel like I should take a few names into the delivery room with me in case you are not a "Cole."

What if I look you in the eyes and your soul screams another name? I guess, you can really look back at this journal and laugh, eh?

Every morning it seems I wake up at 7 o'clock and, for a least an hour, all I can do is lie there and think about becoming a mother and how, in about two weeks, you will be here and my life will be so different.

I am looking forward to it so much, but I'm also scared to death! I really hope I do a good job. I'll try my best! It's all I can do!

## You say "Goodbye" and I say "Hello"

Three months later, after returning home from school one day, Mom called me from work. I could hear the excitement in her voice as she screamed, "Honey, you did it! You're in!"

"What do you mean I'm in? NSCAD! Who told you?" I was a little confused by how she could possibly know this information before me.

"Now don't be upset with me, but I opened your acceptance letter. I was so worried you might not have gotten in that I wanted to be able to break the news to you just in case you had a seizure from the disappointment."

Did she say "acceptance letter?"

Truthfully, I didn't blame her. Before my surgery, I probably would have had a seizure and I could see how challenging it would be for her not to think the worst after the last 19 years.

"Oh, my God, I can't believe it!" I slid slowly down the wall to sit on the floor. My dream had actually come true! All the pain, emptiness and debilitating fear immediately vanished, replaced with pure bliss. So this is what it felt like to succeed. It was a feeling I wanted to experience many times.

Mom told me that, when she found out, she ran to her office and announced it in the hallway that "her little girl was going to art school!"

After watching my mother for years going through endless battles fighting for my education, freedom and praying I would live to see this day, her co-workers gathered in the hallway with a round of applause. It was a truly magical day.

That night, we celebrated over dinner and, as I fell asleep, I couldn't wait to get to school to share my news with my art teacher. Who wouldn't want to tell her art teacher that she got accepted to the second most competitive art program in North America—Emily Carr, in Vancouver, being the first.

As soon as I arrived at the high school I sought her out and finally located her in the school library.

"Miss, you will never guess what I have to tell you?" I tapped her on the shoulder, barely containing my excitement. "I got accepted to NSCAD. Can you believe it?"

What happened next surprised me and was not the reaction I was looking for. She turned to me and, in a dry, arrogant tone responded, "YOU got into NSCAD?" Then she turned away, shaking her head, as if to say, *"Geez they let anyone into that joint."*

I guess I could understand to some degree how she might think that. I was completely uninspired in her class and it was the exact same class I took four years earlier in grade nine, right down to the watercolour sailboat picture. I felt confined in that room, totally zapped of any creative insight.

At the same time, I thought, "What the hell!?"

I mean, wasn't she supposed to be my supporter? Isn't that what teachers do? Well, I guess I should have known better after so many teachers in my life had belittled me, why not one more.

Deflated and heartbroken, I left the library. Maybe it wasn't that big of a deal. Maybe other people just didn't understand how badly I wanted it.

I went to my first class, which was my favorite, English, with Mr. Mac. This teacher was, by far, the one I related to the most. He always had such a spark in the way he taught the material and, after countless years of struggling to remember, I always remembered Mr. Mac's class.

He had a comical way about him that students related to, and whenever we became a little carried away, you could always expect to hear him clap his hand and shout out, "Okay, come on now, kids, let's play school, let's play school."

Mr. Mac was many students' favorite teacher. The fact that he always remembered each student's name, even for years after attending his class, put him on the high-respect list.

I was the first to walk into the classroom, so eager to get to school that morning to share my news. I didn't feel like sharing anymore, too afraid of being shot down again and embarrassed. Taking my regular seat in the corner, I got my books out of my bag and prepared for the arrival of my friends.

"Hey, kid," Mr. Mac said as he smiled at me, "What's new? How are things?"

"Good," I responded, with some hesitancy, not sure if I should tell him about my acceptance or not.

Then, ever so nonchalantly, I finally confessed.

"Well there is this one thing. I did get accepted to NSCAD yesterday."

For the rest of my life, I will never forget the look on Mr. Mac's face. At first it was a look of shock, as if he never expected me to say that. Then it melted into the purest, most gentle expression of gleaming pride as his smile grew to encompass his whole face.

"Cara, that's wonderful news! Way to go, kid. I knew you could do it!"

His words were exactly the confirmation I needed to hear. It was a big deal and Mr. Mac knew it. That was why what he did next stayed in my heart as one of the kindest gestures ever to bless my young life.

As the students began entering the class and sitting in their assigned seats, Mr. Mac began organizing his work on top of his desk. Without looking up he began speaking to the students.

"As you might know, one of our students has experienced a tremendous amount of adversity in the past few years."

"Oh, my God, is he talking about me?" I thought while trying not to turn a thousand shades of red.

Looking up, to meet the eyes of all the young faces looking back at him, he continued, "Her dream of pursuing her goal was not easy, I know this for a fact, but I would like to announce that today Cara Jones has been accepted to the Nova Scotia College of Art and Design!"

You know those moments in life where you feel like you are in a feel-good movie and you can't believe that this scene is actually playing out in your own life? This was definitely one of those moments.

Simultaneously, without direction from Mr. Mac, my classmates all stood and began applauding and cheering in my direction, nodding their heads in joy and approval. I jumped, startled and surprised. I wept joyous tears of gratitude. It was one of the most memorable moments of my life and I will never forget Mr. Mac for making it so.

Two months later, sitting in the school auditorium dressed in a blue gown and cap, I listened as the principal called out each graduate's name as each walked across the stage.

I looked over at my Mom and Dad, sitting with my birth grandparents, Joe and Virginia, and saw the joy radiating from their faces. As my eyes met theirs, I couldn't help but reflect on the concept of miracles. How amazing it is that without them I would not be alive, and how they were sharing this experience with the two people who raised me and adopted me as their own and, without whom, I would also not be alive. They both gave me life, and now they were there to celebrate the moment that so many had deemed impossible. I realized, sitting there, about to take the next step in life—life that was almost taken away from me—that nothing was impossible. I vowed to always remember this and never to let anyone tell me "never" again.

Out of the corner of my eye, I saw a flicker of a light. Suddenly, I felt a hand on my shoulder that was so real I turned around to see who was standing behind me, but only my classmates stared back at me. I whispered, "Did one of you guys just put your hand on my shoulder?" They shook their heads, no. I turned back to face the stage and, after a few minutes, I felt the hand on my shoulder again. This time I had a calm, peaceful sensation and I recognized the feeling. It was Dini. As if the entire room disappeared for a moment, all I could feel was his presence and love for me. I closed my eyes and felt his joy. "Cara Jones," the vice-principal called over the microphone. My eyes opened. The million butterflies fluttering in my stomach helped snap me back into the moment. I made my way towards her and she placed my diploma in one hand, shook my other hand and pulled me into her, whispering, "Cara, you are getting the hell out of here!"

Even though I wanted to laugh, I looked her squarely in the eye and responded, "Damn straight, I am!"

With one foot in front of the other, I savored this moment that I had worked so hard for, and crossed the stage a high school graduate.

# CHAPTER THIRTY-FIVE

# THE BIRTH OF CHANGE

January 18, 2005

Dear Cole

    I started to feel labour symptoms and your due date is just a few days away. These are the last moments I will feel you inside me, kicking, turning and growing. I'm sure I will miss it very much, but I'm so excited to meet you. I lie in bed thinking that these are my last few moments alone, sleeping in, going somewhere on the spur of the moment but, at the same time, I don't really care. I'm just so excited to meet you!

    I hope that you will look back at my story, our story, and know that your mother tried her best to give you the most in life. I hope you understand that no matter what anyone tells you, you can accomplish whatever you set your mind to. My life is a testimony to that. Although I am scared of the unknown, and how I will support you, I also know that I have gotten this far with you by my side so who knows what distances we can reach together.

    I am really afraid of the pain I will feel in labour. You would think that it would be a walk in the park compared to brain surgery. Hopefully it will all go smoothly. I pray that you are healthy and never have to experience an illness like I did. I hope I'm good at discipline, but am fair as well. I pray that God gives me the strength, courage, knowledge and love to be the best mother I can be. I love you so much and I haven't even looked into your eyes yet. I hope you will come early, like tomorrow! Your mother is so impatient.

So, until we meet in person, I will do my best to bring you into this world smoothly. I know that our journey together is just the beginning of what life has to offer, and I hope to instill in you the message that has been instilled in me: never-say-never, always reach for more.

# CHAPTER THIRTY-SIX

# SEVEN YEARS LATER

May 18, 2011

Dear Cole,

Last night you told me about Heaven. We just finished our usual routine of bath, book and bed when you looked up at me with sadness in your eyes, tears forming at the corners. Curling up on my lap I stroked your hair, holding your head close to my heart.

"What's wrong, honey? Tell mommy what's wrong!"

I could feel your heaviness and I couldn't help but empathize; I felt it in my heart too.

"Mommy, I'm sad about Nana and Ottilia, and I don't understand why people keep talking about one Heaven. There is more than one Heaven Mom, I remember, I was there."

With that confession you began to weep. I tried to hold back the tears and felt so horrible that you had to witness such tragedy at such a young age. It had been more than I ever wanted for you to see or experience, but I knew that we could not control what happened, only how we felt about it.

It had only been three short months. In that time, you experienced the death and murder of a friend, you watched her five children grieve their mother, then my boyfriend moved out on us, and now your Nana, your second mother, was paralyzed and in the hospital after a severe stroke. Your whole world had been turned upside down, and so had mine.

I was supposed to finish this book the month before this all took place, but now I feel it is only right that I share this story with you so that you know all that you taught me and all the world taught us, about letting go . . .

CPSIA information can be obtained
at www.ICGtesting.com
Printed in the USA
LVOW08s0447010217
522791LV00001B/56/P